PCs Just the Steps™

FOR

DUMMIES®

2ND EDITION

by Nancy Muir

WILEY

Wiley Publishing, Inc.

PCs Just the Steps™ For Dummies®, 2nd Edition

Published by
Wiley Publishing, Inc.
111 River Street
Hoboken, NJ 07030-5774

www.wiley.com

Copyright © 2009 by Wiley Publishing, Inc., Indianapolis, Indiana

Published by Wiley Publishing, Inc., Indianapolis, Indiana

Published simultaneously in Canada

For general information on our other products and services, please contact our Customer Care Department within the U.S. at 877-762-2974, outside the U.S. at 317-572-3993, or fax 317-572-4002.

For technical support, please visit www.wiley.com/techsupport.

Wiley also publishes its books in a variety of electronic formats. Some content that appears in print may not be available in electronic books.

Library of Congress Control Number: 2009920035

ISBN: 978-0-470-40692-2

Manufactured in the United States of America

10 9 8 7 6 5 4 3 2 1

WILEY

About the Author

Nancy Muir has written over 50 books on technology and business topics including *Microsoft Office Project 2007 For Dummies* and *Staying Safe Online For Seniors For Dummies* (both by Wiley Publishing, Inc.). Nancy has taught Internet safety and technical writing at the university level and holds a certificate in distance learning design from The University of Washington. She is currently the Director of Content Development for LOOK**BOTH**WAYS, Inc., an Internet safety company.

Dedication

To my fantastic husband Earl for all his love and support. And to my late father-in-law Dick Boysen, who was a wonderful example of how to live life to the fullest.

Author's Acknowledgments

I want to thank Greg Croy for entrusting me with many book projects over the years. Happy retirement! And thanks to my editor Blair Pottenger. (You're the best.) Thanks also to Virginia Sanders for copyediting my words so they make sense and to Lee Musick for a great technical edit.

Publisher's Acknowledgments

We're proud of this book; please send us your comments through our online registration form located at http://dummies.custhelp.com. For other comments, please contact our Customer Care Department within the U.S. at 877-762-2974, outside the U.S. at 317-572-3993, or fax 317-572-4002.

Some of the people who helped bring this book to market include the following:

Acquisitions and Editorial

Project Editor: Blair J. Pottenger

Executive Acquisitions Editor: Greg Croy

Copy Editor: Virginia Sanders

Technical Editor: Lee Musick

Editorial Manager: Kevin Kirschner

Editorial Assistant: Amanda Foxworth

Sr. Editorial Assistant: Cherie Case

Cartoons: Rich Tennant (www.the5thwave.com)

Composition Services

Project Coordinator: Katie Key

Layout and Graphics: Carl Byers, Carrie A. Cesavice, Jennifer Mayberry, Jill A. Proll, Christine Williams

Proofreaders: Laura Albert, Cindy Lee Ballew/Precisely Write

Indexer: Broccoli Information Management

Publishing and Editorial for Technology Dummies

 Richard Swadley, Vice President and Executive Group Publisher

 Andy Cummings, Vice President and Publisher

 Mary Bednarek, Executive Acquisitions Director

 Mary C. Corder, Editorial Director

Publishing for Consumer Dummies

 Diane Graves Steele, Vice President and Publisher

Composition Services

 Gerry Fahey, Vice President of Production Services

 Debbie Stailey, Director of Composition Services

Contents at a Glance

Computers have come a long way in just 20 years or so. They're now at the heart of the way many people communicate, shop, and learn. They provide useful tools for tracking information, organizing finances, and being creative.

Whether you're a young person just getting your first computer, or a senior who is finally getting around to discovering all that computers can enable you to do, or anybody in between, this book will ease you into the world of computers quickly and painlessly.

About This Book

This book is for people who are new to using a computer and want to discover the basics of making settings, working with files and folders, getting on the Internet, and maintaining and protecting a Windows Vista–based computer. *Just the Steps* books provide just that: just the steps you need to complete common computer procedures quickly without a lot of explanation to slow you down.

Foolish Assumptions

This book is organized by sets of tasks. These tasks start from the very beginning, assuming you know little about computers, and they guide you through from the most basic steps in easy-to-understand language. Because I assume you're new to computers, the book provides explanations or definitions of technical terms to help you out.

Introduction

Conventions used in this book

➡ When you have to type something in a text box, I put it in **bold** type. Whenever I mention a Web site address, I put it in another font, `like this`.

➡ For menu commands, I use the ➪ symbol to separate menu choices. For example, choose Tools➪Internet Options. The ➪ symbol is just my way of saying "Open the Tools menu and then click Internet Options."

➡ Callouts for figures draw your attention to an action you need to perform. In some cases, points of interest in a figure might be circled. The text tells you what to look for, the circle makes it easy to find.

 This icon points out insights or helpful suggestions related to the tasks in the step list.

All computers are run by software called an *operating system,* such as Windows. Because Microsoft Windows–based personal computers (PCs) are the most common type, the book focuses mostly on Windows functionality and specifically on the latest version of Windows, Windows Vista.

Why You Need This Book

Working with computers can be a daunting prospect to people who have little experience with them. One-thousand-page reference books could send you running for the hills. However, with the simple step-by-step approach of this book, you can get up to speed with computers and overcome any technophobia you might have experienced.

You can work through this book from beginning to end or simply open up a chapter to solve a problem or help you learn a new skill whenever you need it. The steps in each task get you where you want to go quickly, without a lot of technical explanation. In no time, you'll start picking up the skills you need to become a confident computer user.

After you've finished this book, you'll know your way around a PC and you'll probably want to start using some specific applications. For that, I recommend other *For Dummies* books such as *Word 2007 For Dummies* by Dan Gookin, *Microsoft Office Project 2007 For Dummies* (by yours truly), or *Quicken 2009 For Dummies* by Stephen L. Nelson (all by Wiley Publishing, Inc.).

How This Book Is Organized

This book is conveniently divided into several handy parts to help you find what you need.

➥ **Part I: Setting Up Your Computer:** If you need to get started with the basics of using a computer, this part is for you. These chapters help you understand all the parts and technologies that make up your computer, and explore how to set up your computer out of the box, including hooking it up to devices such as a printer and working with settings for input devices like your mouse and keyboard. These chapters provide information for exploring the Windows desktop when you first turn on your computer, and working with your mouse, keyboard, monitor, and disc drives. Finally, I provide information on setting up accessibility features that help you if you need to adapt Windows to work better for you if you have a visual, hearing, or hand strength issue (like arthritis).

➥ **Part II: Getting to Know Windows:** Here's where you start working with the Windows Vista operating system. You deal with basic settings such as your computer's date and time setting, set up a password to protect your data, explore the Windows desktop, and discover how to get help when you need it. This is also the part where you find out how to customize the look of Windows.

➡ **Part III: Getting to Work:** Windows allows you to organize the data you create in files and folders, and the first chapter in this part gets you up to speed on file and folder management. Next you explore the world of software, even practicing a bit with some built-in Windows software to write a document and edit a picture. This is the part where you find out about network basics, in case you want to set up your own home network to enable two or more computers to access devices such as a printer or to get on the Internet. Chapters in this part also introduce you to some multimedia devices and settings so you can work with sounds and images, and set up peripherals — devices such as printers, scanners, and faxes that help you share information in your computer with others.

➡ **Part IV: Going Online:** It's time to get online! The chapters in this part help you understand what the Internet is and what tools and functions it makes available to you. Find out how to explore the Internet with a Web browser; how to stay in touch with people via e-mail, instant messaging, chat, blogs; and even how to make Internet phone calls.

➡ **Part V: Computer Maintenance and Security:** Now that you have a computer, you have certain responsibilities towards it (just like having a child or puppy!). In this case, you need to protect the data on your computer, which you can do using a program called Windows Defender. In addition, you need to perform some routine maintenance tasks to keep your hard drive uncluttered and virus free.

Get Going!

Whether you need to start from square one and set up your computer or you're ready to just start enjoying the tools and toys your current computer makes available, it's time to get going, get online, and get computer savvy.

Part I

Setting Up Your Computer

The 5th Wave   By Rich Tennant

"I'm ordering our new PC. Do you want it left-brain or right-brain oriented?"

Getting to Know Computer Basics

Chapter 1

*U*sing a computer is actually pretty simple, but understanding the various technologies that make up a computer is a little harder. You don't have to know how to build a computer, but to choose the right computer for your needs or talk intelligently with the clerk in the computer store or technical support, it helps to have a basic understanding.

In this chapter, you educate yourself about

➡ How data is stored on your hard drive

➡ What an operating system does

➡ Various computer configurations available such as desktops and laptops

➡ The value of wireless capability in your computer to keep you connected

➡ The various features offered in monitors that may make your computing life easier on the eyes

➡ Various options for storing your data

➡ What, exactly, a microprocessor is and which is the best one for you

Get ready to . . .

Examine Your Hard Drive

Your computer can have several drives. All but the hard drive are external and typically plug into your computer via a USB port. The hard drive is also called a hard disk. It's essentially a platter inside your computer where your computer stores programs and data.

Here are some important-to-know facts about your hard drive:

➠ **A hard drive uses magnetic recording to store data.** This is similar to old-style recording tape. You can write data to your hard drive as a series of bytes, use that data, and erase it. However, be aware that the magnetic pattern on your hard drive can retain erased data even after you've erased it.

➠ **Your hard drive is divided into** *sectors* **that include several tracks.** Every sector contains a set number of bytes. Typical sectors are 256 or 512 bytes. Formatting a hard drive creates this sector and track structure, along with a file allocation table that helps your computer retrieve data.

➠ **Similar to an old record player's stylus, a computer hard drive works with an arm containing read/write heads.** These heads move over the hard drive as it spins to locate various bytes of information.

➠ **Hard drives come with different capacities for storing data.** Today most are measured in gigabytes (GB). The higher the gigabytes, the more data your computer can store, so check computer manufacturer specs (see Figure 1-1) before you buy.

Figure 1-1: Manufacturer specs for memory and hard drive capacity

If you're not sure what capacity your hard drive has you can check your computer manufacturer's specifications. You'll find these in your user manual or go to the manufacturer's Web site and search for your model. You can also choose Start➪Control Panel➪System and Maintenance and click the View Amount of RAM and Processor Speed link to see your model name, RAM, and processor speed.

Understand Operating Systems

Operating systems (OSes) are software programs, such as Windows or the Macintosh OS, that run your computer. Your computer comes with an operating system pre-installed. An operating system runs your applications and allows you to manage files on your computer and protect your data.

Here are some things you should know about operating systems:

➡ **Tools:** Operating systems often come with extra tools and features to help you get your work done, such as calculators (see Figure 1-2), games, tools to help users with vision or hearing disabilities, and programs to protect your computer from viruses.

➡ **Incompatibilities:** Today, many operating systems allow you to use files created with other operating systems seamlessly, but there are still some incompatibilities. You may need to download converters to be able to open files created on a computer using one operating system on a computer using another.

➡ **Upgrades:** Over time new operating systems come out and you may reach a point where you want to upgrade your OS. Most offer frequent interim updates you can download for free, but when a new version of the product is released, you'll have to buy an upgrade package to begin using the newest features.

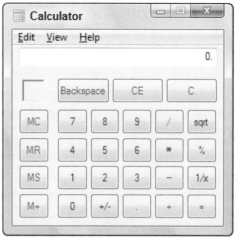

Figure 1-2: Windows' Calculator

 Security features of operating systems such as Windows Defender are getting more and more robust, and it's important that you take advantage of them to protect your data. However in many cases you have to enable these features for them to do any good. See Chapter 20 for more about computer security.

Choose the Right Computer

There are different styles of computers available. To help you choose the best computer for your needs, here are some styles to consider:

➠ **A desktop computer** (see Figure 1-3) is meant to stay at one location. It can take the form of a tower that you place on your desk or the floor with a separate monitor. Other models are designed so the monitor contains the guts of the computer, as with some Macintosh models.

➠ **A laptop or notebook computer** (see Figure 1-4) is more portable than a desktop, though these currently run the gamut from four pounds or so to heftier desktop models weighing in at nine pounds or more. With a laptop, the monitor is built into a chassis that also contains the keyboard and a built-in mouse that usually takes the form of a touch pad or touch button.

➠ **A Tablet PC** is a Windows computer that allows you to interact with the computer by "writing" on the screen or making choices using a stylus. Tablet PCs can lay flat, allowing you to use them like a pad or tablet.

 Netbooks are like laptops, except that they have limited functionality. Essentially they allow you to surf the Internet and retrieve e-mail but not run other software programs. Because of their limited feature set, they aren't really considered PCs.

Figure 1-3: Desktops take up more space

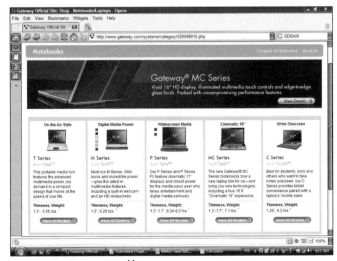

Figure 1-4: Laptops are portable

Look at Wireless Capabilities

If you own a computer with wireless capabilities, you can connect to the Internet without plugging your computer into a cable connection or phone line. You can go online using a wireless card or device in your computer and an Internet access point in your home network or even use access points in many public locations such as airports and hotels.

Here are the basics about wireless connections:

➡ **Subscriptions:** You can subscribe to a Wireless Wide Area Network offered by companies such as Verizon (see Figure 1-5) and then pick up their signal as you move around.

➡ **Hotspots:** You can pick up public connections called *hotspots* (see Figure 1-6) at locations such as hotels and coffee shops. Some public locations charge a fee, but many others offer a wireless connection (also called Wi-Fi) for free.

➡ **Wireless home networks:** You can set up a wireless network in your home and access it from several computers located throughout your house after you've configured them to access the network.

➡ **Wireless protocols:** Check your computer's specifications to see what wireless protocol it uses. A popular wireless protocol is Bluetooth, referred to as 802.11, which you'll see associated with letters such as a, b, g, and n. Wireless version n is the latest and boosts your reception range significantly over earlier versions.

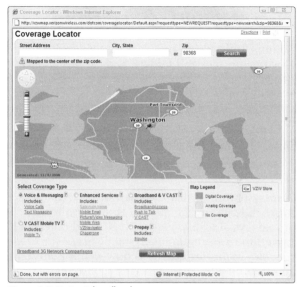

Figure 1-5: Verizon's broadband access map

Figure 1-6: Find directories of hotspots online

Select a Monitor

Your monitor displays your operating system environment, online documents, files and folders, and various applications you use to get your work done. Because you may look at your monitor many hours a day, it's important that you understand how monitor size and display quality affect your viewing experience.

➠ **Sizes:** Monitors come in sizes ranging from very small 8.6-inch netbooks (see Figure 1-7) to huge 24-inch desktop models (see Figure 1-8).

➠ **Displays:** Monitor displays use various technologies that afford different image quality. Some monitors use LCD (liquid crystal display) technologies and others use TFT (thin film transfer) liquid crystal display. One of the variables in display quality is how well it keeps crisp images no matter what the lighting around it.

➠ **Screen resolutions:** Screen resolution relates to the crispness of the image on your monitor screen. The higher the resolution numbers, the sharper your display image.

The monitor you choose depends on the type of computer you get (laptop where smaller size may be important for portability versus desktop); what activities you use your computer for (if you use lots of graphics applications or games, you might prefer a monitor with a higher-end graphics card); and any vision challenges you may face (in which case you might want a larger monitor).

Figure 1-7: Portable computers may sport very small monitors

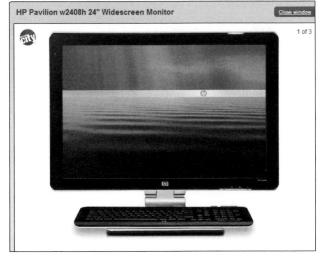

Figure 1-8: A large display helps with games and graphics applications

Understand Data Storage

You can store data to your computer hard drive or store it on other media. In fact, it's a good idea to keep a copy of your important files on other media in case your computer hard drive gets damaged or wears out. Here are several types of data storage:

➡ **CDs and DVDS** are hard plastic disks that you can use to store data and read it. Your computer has a CD/DVD drive which looks like a slot that you slip the disk into.

➡ **Flash drives** are sticks, about the dimensions of a very thick piece of gum (see Figure 1-9), that slide into a USB (universal serial bus) slot. These have capacities up to and exceeding 8 gigabytes, so they can hold lots of files.

➡ **External hard drives** (see Figure 1-10) usually plug into a USB port in your computer. They range in size from a bit larger than a deck of cards to a paperback book, and essentially they give you a second hard drive to back up to.

 Netbooks, which are very small laptops that are becoming popular for their portability, don't have CD/DVD drives. To access CD/DVD content for these consider downloading software from the Internet, sharing a CD/DVD drive of a larger computer over a network, or getting an external CD/DVD drive.

Figure 1-9: A USB stick

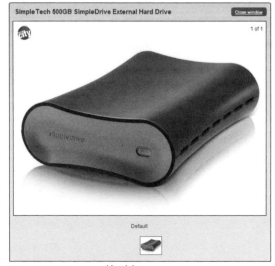

Figure 1-10: An external hard drive

Understand Microprocessors

Microprocessors, also simply called *processors,* are what enable your computer to run and process data. Microprocessors are computer chips which include integrated circuits.

Here are some things to consider about microprocessors when you're buying a new computer:

➡ **Brand:** The two key players in manufacturing processors today are Intel (see Figure 1-11) and AMD. When you buy a computer and you prefer one brand to another, check the models to see which they use.

➡ **Speed:** Microprocessor clock speed ratings, given in gigahertz, determine how fast your computer runs. You'll pay more for a faster microprocessor, but if you use your computer quite a bit, especially for applications such as graphics and games, the speed may be worth the price.

➡ **Power management:** Laptop computers have power management issues that make the choice of processor even more important. For example, the Core 2 Duo processor from Intel uses less power than its predecessors.

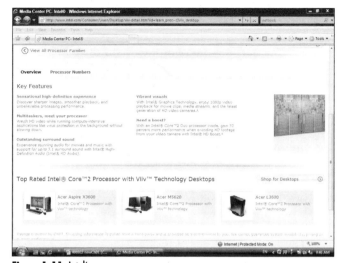

Figure 1-11: Intel's processors

 One other thing to think about is chip cores. In the latest chips the processor 'brain' is divided up into different logic sectors called cores. This helps speed up your computer by allowing it to perform multiple tasks at the same time. For example, you might buy a laptop Core2 Duo processor, which has two cores, or spring for a high end desktop with a Quad Core chip (4 cores).

Your PC Out of the Box

Your desktop computer might be housed in a big metal container (called a *tower*) that you keep on the floor under your desk, or it might be a single unit built into your monitor or even a portable laptop. It is likely to have multiple slots and places to plug in things (these are called *ports*) as well as indicator lights that tell you things like when the power is on or off.

When you get your PC and take it out of the box, there's likely to be a handy piece of paper that tells you what to plug in where so you can connect your monitor, keyboard, and mouse. Most computers come with color-coded plugs to make it easy to spot where a particular item plugs in. Still, a basic overview of what's on your PC, how you turn your computer on and off, and how you get around the Windows Vista desktop (the central command center of Windows) may be helpful.

Although computer models differ somewhat, the information and illustrations in this chapter can help you locate various switches and connectors on your own computer.

If you've never worked with a PC before, use the tasks in this chapter to do the following:

➡ **Locate connections on the front and back of your computer:** You use these connections to attach a power plug, your monitor, printer, mouse, keyboard, and more to your central processing unit (CPU in computer speak).

➡ **Turn on your computer, work with the Start menu, get around the Windows Vista desktop, and turn off your computer:** This is your first introduction to booting up, using, and logging off of your computer.

Chapter

2

Get ready to . . .

Locate Switches and Plug In Things

Use this table in tandem with Figure 2-1 to locate device-to-PC connector ports. Note that many devices use a USB connector these days; so, for example, if you have a mouse with a USB connector, just plug it into one of your USB ports.

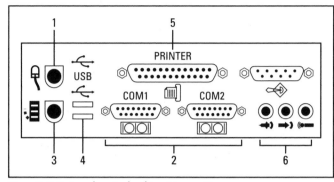

Figure 2-1: Various places to plug things into your PC

Connection	Location	What It's Good For
Mouse	1	Connect your wired mouse
Video Connection	2	Connect your non-USB monitor
Keyboard	3	Connect your wired keyboard
USB ports	4	Connect any USB device
Parallel port	5	Connect to a non-USB printer
Audio	6	Connect speakers

 Note that some monitors and laptop computers have built-in speakers so you don't have to connect separate speakers through the audio port. Discover more about working with sound settings in Chapter 14.

 Not every computer will have the same number or type of ports. For example, newer computers use USB ports for connecting a wide variety of devices, from printers to digital cameras or a wireless mouse. Older computers have fewer USB ports available, but newer ones are likely to offer 4 or 5.

Turn On Your Computer and Log On to Windows

1. With your computer set up, you're ready to turn it on. Start by pressing the power button on your computer to begin the Windows Vista start-up sequence.

2. If this is the first time you've started your computer, you see a screen that guides you through initial setup, which usually includes items such as specifying your country, date and time, and username. Also, your computer manufacturer might have added further setup steps, such as registering your computer via the Internet.

3. In the following Windows Vista Welcome screen, all user accounts are represented by labeled picture icons. Click the account you want to access.

4. In the following screen, enter your password if you have assigned one and then click the arrow button (or click the Switch User button to return to the previous screen and choose another user to log on as). Windows Vista verifies your password and displays the Windows Vista desktop, as shown in Figure 2-2.

 If you haven't set up the password protection feature when you click an account icon on the Welcome screen, you're taken directly to the Windows Vista desktop. You can find out more about adding and changing passwords in Chapter 7.

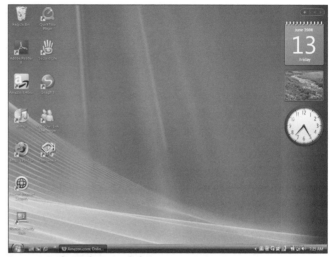

Figure 2-2: The Windows Vista desktop

 To log out from one user account and log in with another, choose Start➪Log Off. This takes you to the Log Off screen, where you can click any other user's icon to log on through that account.

 If this is the very first time you've turned on a new computer, your manufacturer may have included an introductory series of screens to make certain settings for how your computer will work. See your computer documentation for an explanation of these options.

Work with the Start Menu

1. One of the ways you can locate and work with installed software and files is through the Start menu. Press the Windows key on your keyboard or click the Start button on the desktop to display the Start menu.

2. From the Start menu, you can do any of the following:

   • Click the Recent Items choice on the right of the Start menu to see files you've worked with most recently. (See Figure 2-3.)

   • Click All Programs to display a list of all software installed on your computer. You can click any program in the list to open it or click a program folder to see more options.

   • Click any category in the upper-right section of the Start menu to display a Windows Explorer window with related folders and files (such as the Music folder shown in Figure 2-4).

   • Click the Power Button icon to put the computer to sleep but keep current programs running, or click the Lock icon to go to the log on screen; if your account requires a password to open it, only somebody who knows the password can now open Windows.

   • Click the arrow next to the Lock icon to display a menu of choices for shutting down or restarting your computer, for logging off, or for logging in as a different user.

3. When you move your cursor away from the Start menu and click your mouse or press Esc on your keyboard, the menu disappears.

 If you open the Start menu and right-click in a blank area of the menu, a shortcut menu pops up. Choose Properties to display the Taskbar and Start Menu Properties dialog box, where you can customize the Start menu behavior. If you would rather use the look and feel of the Start menu in older versions of Windows, select Classic Start Menu in the Taskbar and Start Menu Properties dialog box and then click OK. (Note that this book deals only with the Windows Vista–style Start menu features.)

Figure 2-3: The Start menu

Figure 2-4: Windows Explorer

Navigate the Windows Desktop

1. With the Windows Vista desktop displayed (see Figure 2-5) do any of the following:

   - Double-click a shortcut icon to open that program, folder, or document.

   - Right-click an item to display a shortcut menu (see Figure 2-6) for commonly performed tasks such as Open, Send To, or Copy.

2. Move your mouse to the bottom of the screen to display the Windows Vista taskbar if it's not already displayed. Do any of the following:

   - Click a window button for a running application to maximize it.

   - Click items in the notification area (on the right side of the taskbar) to see the current date and time, or to access other special Windows Vista programs. Some items here just display information when you hover your mouse over them; others can be double-clicked to open a window with more options or information.

   - Click a button on the Quick Launch bar (on the left side of the taskbar) to quickly start various programs.

3. Click the Start button to open the Start menu (see the previous task for more information).

    Windows Vista has some preset desktop icons, such as the Recycle Bin (the place where Windows places deleted files and folders), and your computer manufacturer probably placed several icons on the desktop for preinstalled programs and tools. You can also create your own shortcuts; see Chapter 8 for more about this procedure.

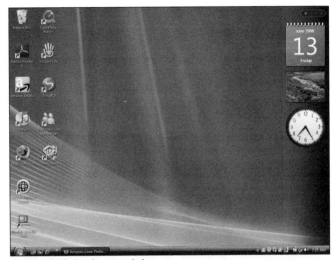

Figure 2-5: The Windows Vista desktop

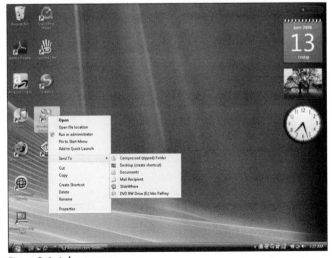

Figure 2-6: A shortcut menu

Turn Off Your Computer

1. To turn off your computer, you should initiate a shut down sequence in your operating system rather than simply turning off the power. Click the Start button.

2. In the bottom-right corner of the Start menu, click the arrow to the right of the button with a lock on it.

3. In the resulting sub-menu, as shown in Figure 2-7, choose Shut Down. Windows Vista closes, and the computer turns off. Turning off your computer through the shut down process helps your computer close out of any processes it's doing behind the scenes so you don't lose data or settings.

 You can also choose Restart to turn off and then immediately turn on your computer. You would use this setting if your computer is having problems and you want your system to reset or if you install new software or make new settings and are instructed to restart your computer.

 The Sleep option on the shortcut menu in Step 2 is like letting your computer take a nap. The screen goes dark, and in the case of laptops, power consumption lowers. By clicking your mouse button or pressing Enter on your keyboard, you can wake up your computer again with everything just as you left it.

Figure 2-7: Various options for shutting down your computer

 When you turn off your computer, peripherals such as your monitor or printer don't turn off automatically. You have to press their power buttons to turn each off manually.

Using Discs and Drives

*T*he motherboard of your computer is where all the circuitry for your PC lives. The motherboard also contains the processor chip that runs your computer. Your hard drive is connected to the motherboard. This hard drive (typically designated as the C drive) is the main physical storage area for your PC.

You can also use removable media drives — such a CD-ROM drive, a DVD drive, or a flash drive — to give your computer access to additional data and storage. Your computer can then read files from that media as well as write files to it, if the media is formatted as writable. CDs and DVDs are flat discs that slide into a slim drawer somewhere on your computer; flash drives are small "sticks" that slot into any USB drive.

Of course, you need a way to view and work with all that data, wherever it's stored. In this chapter, you explore your drives, including the following:

➡ Locating files with Windows Explorer

➡ Inserting and ejecting various types of storage media

➡ Checking the memory on a drive

➡ Adding memory

➡ Placing a drive icon on the desktop for ease of access

➡ Initializing a new hard drive

➡ Partitioning a hard drive

Get ready to . . .

View Files with Windows Explorer

1. Windows Explorer is a program you can use to find a file or folder on any drive by navigating through an outline of folders and subfolders. To get started, right-click the Start menu and choose Explore.

2. In the resulting Windows Explorer window, shown in Figure 3-1, double-click a folder in the Folders list on the left to open the folder.

3. The folder's contents are displayed in a pane on the right side of the window. If necessary, open a series of folders in this right pane until you locate the file you want.

4. When the file you want appears in the list of items in the Name column in the right pane, double-click its icon to open it.

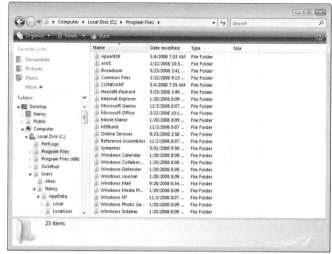

Figure 3-1: Finding files and folders in Windows Explorer

 To see different perspectives and information about files in Windows Explorer, click the arrow on the Views button at the top (it looks like a series of columns) and choose one of the following menu options: Extra Large, Large, Medium, or Small Icons for graphical displays; Details to show details such as Date Modified and Size; and Tiles to show the file/folder name, type, and size. If you're working with a folder containing graphics files, the graphics automatically display as thumbnails unless you choose Details.

 You can open commonly used folders from the Start menu, including Documents, Pictures, and Music. Click one of these, and Windows Explorer opens that particular window.

Insert and Eject a CD or DVD

1. Locate your CD/DVD drive. You usually open the drive by pressing a button on the front of the drive and close it again by pressing the same button.

2. A dialog box appears (see Figure 3-2), offering different options for working with the files on the disc. To view the files on the disc, click Open Folder to View Files.

3. In the resulting Windows Explorer window (see Figure 3-3), you can double-click files to open them or save files to the disc. (See Chapter 11 for more about backing up files to disc.)

4. When you're finished with the disc, right-click the drive name on the list on the left side of the Windows Explorer window and choose Eject to eject it.

 Ejecting works a bit differently on a Mac. Click the Finder icon to open the Finder. Click on the disc name on the left side of this window, and then click File⇨Eject "File Name".

Figure 3-2: The AutoPlay menu

Figure 3-3: An overview of all the disc contents

Insert and Remove a USB Flash Drive

1. Locate an unused USB slot on your computer. (On desktop towers, this slot might be in the front or back; in laptops, it's usually on the sides or back.)

2. Slip the flash drive into the USB slot. A dialog box appears, offering different options for working with the files on the disc. To view the files on the flash drive, click Open Folder to View Files.

3. In the resulting Windows Explorer window (see Figure 3-4), you can double-click files to open them or save files to the flash drive. (See Chapter 11 for more about backing up files.)

4. When you've finished with the flash drive, click the taskbar icon labeled Safely Eject Hardware and choose the flash drive on the pop-up list that appears. A window appears, telling you it's okay to remove the flash drive (see Figure 3-5). Pull it out of the slot gently and tuck it in a safe place.

 If you have trouble inserting the flash drive into a USB port try turning it over — it only goes in with the contacts pointing up.

Figure 3-4: Windows Explorer showing all files and folders on a flash drive

Figure 3-5: Removing a flash drive safely

Check Installed Memory

1. Choose Start➪Computer.

2. In the resulting Computer window, right-click the C: disk icon to open a shortcut menu (see Figure 3-6) and then choose Properties.

3. In the resulting Local Disk (C:) Properties dialog box, click the General tab to view the total memory (see Figure 3-7).

4. Click the Close button to close the dialog box.

 When you purchase a computer you will find hard drive capacities such as 120 GB, 250 GB, and 320 GB. GB stands for gigabytes, which represents 1 billion bytes of computer storage. It wasn't that long ago that computer hard drives were measured in kilobytes (1 thousand bytes) so today's extra large hard drives are likely to provide plenty of space for all your computer activities to run.

Figure 3-6: Right-click the C: disk icon

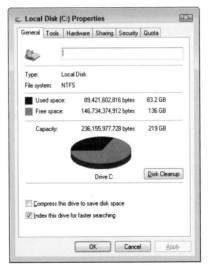

Figure 3-7: The System Properties dialog box

Add Memory

1. To install a memory module, turn off your desktop computer and disconnect all power and other cables from it.

2. Open the PC chassis (see Figure 3-8). Check your user's manual for this procedure, which usually involves removing a few screws and popping the cover off your tower.

3. Touch a metal object with your hand to discharge any static before you reach inside the computer.

4. Locate the slots for memory modules. There are typically three or four in a group. Again, check your manual for the exact location in your PC.

 There are different models of memory modules. Dual Inline Memory Modules (DIMM) are a common type of memory module, and they come with many recent PCs. Check your manufacturer's documentation for your computer to be sure which type of memory module you should be using.

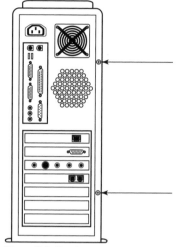

Figure 3-8: Opening your computer

5. If you're replacing an old memory module with a new one, remove the old module first. If your system has clips at either end of the slot, move them to the unlocked position first. If you're adding a memory module, you can simply use an empty slot. See your user's manual to determine which slots make sense for the size of the memory module you're inserting.

6. Remove the new memory module from its sealed bag. Handling the module by its edges, line it up with the slot and insert it firmly but gently (see Figure 3-9). If your computer model requires it, snap the clips in place to hold the module in.

7. Make sure that you didn't disconnect any wires or leave any loose screws inside the PC chassis. Then replace the computer cover and reinsert the screws.

8. Plug the computer in and turn it on. Your computer should sense the new memory when it starts up.

 Warning: Never force any memory module into a slot. Doing so can damage the module or your PC. If the module won't insert easily, you might be holding it the wrong way. Try reversing it, and insert it again.

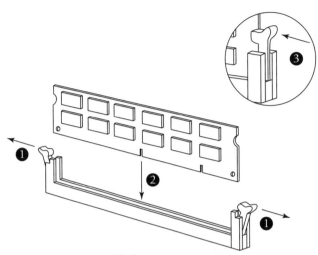

Figure 3-9: A memory module slot

Add a Desktop Shortcut to a Removable Storage Device

1. You may want to frequently access contents of a removable flash drive or DVD, so you may want to create a shortcut for one of these drives on your desktop. Choose Start⇨Computer.

2. In the resulting Computer window, right-click the removable storage drive you want and choose Create Shortcut from the menu that appears (see Figure 3-10). The shortcut is created and placed on the desktop.

 If you like to play audio DVDs frequently, one option is to put a shortcut for the DVD drive on your desktop. However, most modern keyboards offer you keys to start, stop, pause, and even skip to other tracks of your audio DVD. On laptops, these may be function keys that require you to press an fn key and then a function key. On larger keyboards, there may be dedicated keys for controlling audio playback.

 If you use a flash drive all the time to store files, sort of like a second hard drive, it might be a good idea to put that drive icon on your desktop so you can quickly access frequently used files.

Figure 3-10: Create a shortcut for a removable disc

Initialize a New Hard Drive

1. After installing a new hard drive (see your user's manual for instructions, which will vary by system), choose Start⇨Control Panel⇨System and Maintenance.

2. In the resulting System and Maintenance window click Administrative Tools. In the resulting Administrative Tools windows double-click Computer Management, and then click Disk Management in the Computer Management window that appears.

3. In the resulting Disk Management window (see Figure 3-11), right-click the new drive and then choose Initialize Disk.

4. In the resulting Initialize Disk dialog box select the disk to initialize and click OK.

 After you initialize a new hard drive, you should also follow the procedure to partition it (see the following task). The New Partition Wizard you access for that task takes you through partitioning and formatting the drive. For your hard drive, during that procedure, you should format the drive as the primary partition and use all the space on the drive.

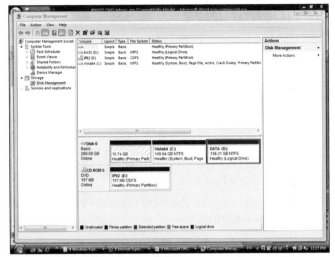

Figure 3-11: The Disk Management window

Partition a Disk

1. Choose Start⇨Control Panel⇨System and Maintenance⇨ Administrative Tools.

2. In the resulting Administrative Tools window, double-click the Computer Management link.

3. In the resulting Computer Management window (as shown in Figure 3-12), click Disk Management in the left pane, right-click a basic disk in the right pane (this is usually your hard drive) that isn't allocated, and then choose New Partition.

4. Follow the steps in the New Partition Wizard to create the new partition.

 A new partition can free up some memory and make your system utilize memory more efficiently. But just so you know, you have to be logged on as a system administrator to complete the steps listed here. If you are an individual desktop user, check settings under User Accounts in the Control Panel to set up administrator status. If you're on a network, ask your network administrator about these rights.

Figure 3-12: The Computer Management window

Setting Up Your Display

Chapter

4

Your monitor is your window into the world of your computer. It's where you view all the data and images your PC stores and manipulates. Essentially three elements are involved in what you see on your monitor screen: the monitor itself, the graphics card installed in your CPU, and the *driver* (that is, software) that controls your monitor.

In addition to these three items, it's important to know how to make settings to fine-tune your display so it's easy on your eyes, especially if you work on your computer many hours every day.

To customize your display, you can do the following:

➡ Adjust settings for your monitor and display. Windows Vista provides settings that you can use to enable your monitor and control the driver.

➡ Add a new graphics card to provide up-to-date capabilities for your display.

➡ Control various features, such as how often the screen image refreshes.

Get ready to . . .

Enable a Monitor

1. If you want to, you can switch monitors and enable one that's currently disabled (for example, to use a larger desktop monitor with your laptop). Connect the monitor to your computer. Right-click the desktop and choose Personalize from the resulting menu.

2. In the Personalization dialog box that appears, click the Display Settings link.

3. In the Display Settings dialog box that appears, click the Advanced Settings button.

4. In the Advanced dialog box (see Figure 4-1), click the Monitor tab and then click the Properties button.

5. On the Driver tab of the Monitor Properties dialog box (see Figure 4-2), click the Enable button.

6. Click OK three times to close all dialog boxes and save the new setting.

 A monitor should be disabled only if it's causing system problems. A Plug and Play monitor should be enabled automatically when you install its driver and plug it in. If you have cause to disable the monitor, you can use this procedure to enable it again.

Figure 4-1: The Advanced Monitor Settings dialog box

Figure 4-2: The Monitor Properties dialog box

Update Your Monitor Driver

1. Right-click the desktop and choose Personalize from the resulting menu.

2. In the Personalization dialog box that appears, click the Display Settings link.

3. In the Display dialog box that appears, click the Advanced Settings button.

4. In the Advanced Settings dialog box, click the Monitor tab and then click the Properties button.

5. On the Driver tab (see Figure 4-3) of the resulting Monitor Properties dialog box, click the Update Driver button.

6. In the Update Driver Software dialog box that appears (see Figure 4-4), choose Search Automatically for Updated Driver Software. This feature searches your computer for any drivers in Windows or on disk and then searches the manufacturer's Web site for updated drivers.

7. The resulting dialog box shows a progress bar indicating that your computer is searching for updated software.

8. In the final window that appears, you're told either that your existing driver is the most current or than an updated driver exists. Click Close.

9. Click OK three times to close all other dialog boxes and save the new setting.

Figure 4-3: The Driver tab of the Monitor Properties dialog box

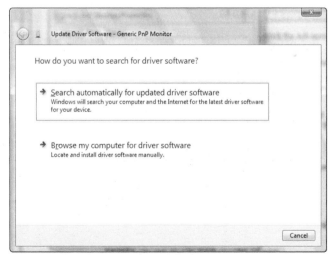

Figure 4-4: The Update Driver Software dialog box

Install a New Graphics Card

1. First, uninstall the existing graphics card driver by using the Uninstall a Program link in the Control Panel. (See Chapter 11 for more about removing software.)

2. Shut off your computer and unplug it. Also shut off any peripherals attached to it, such as a printer, and disconnect your monitor from the CPU (computer body).

3. Remove your CPU cover following the directions in your computer manual. Before touching anything inside the CPU, touch a piece of metal to get rid of any static discharge.

4. Locate the current graphics card (using your manual if necessary) and remove it (see Figure 4-5). This might involve unscrewing the card with a Philips screwdriver.

5. Position the new graphics card over the slot and insert it firmly but gently (see Figure 4-6). If you removed a card-holder screw in Step 4, replace it.

6. Replace the computer cover and plug your monitor back in. Turn on your monitor and then your computer. Your computer automatically detects the new card and displays the Found New Hardware Wizard. Follow its directions to install the new driver.

 Whenever you open your computer case, be very careful about static discharge, which can harm you and the delicate electronics in your computer. Consider wearing an antistatic wristband, which you can get at most electronics stores. Also, to cut down on static, stand on a rubber mat rather than on shag carpet. Finally, occasionally touch a piece of metal to discharge any static in your body.

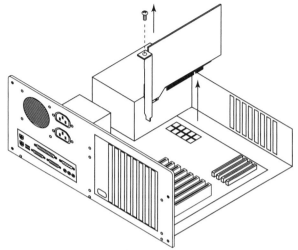

Figure 4-5: Removing a graphics card

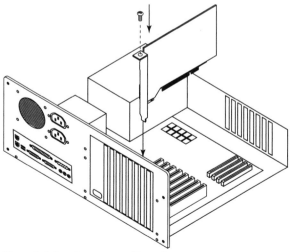

Figure 4-6: Inserting a new graphics card

Adjust Your Computer's Refresh Rate

1. Right-click the desktop and choose Personalize from the resulting menu.

2. In the Personalization window dialog box that appears, click the Display Settings link.

3. In the Display Settings dialog box that appears, click the Monitor tab (see Figure 4-7).

4. Click the DPI Setting arrow and select Normal Size or Large Size.

5. A message box appears, explaining that any changes to fonts will appear after they are installed and the computer is restarted. Click OK to close the message.

6. Click OK to save the setting and close the dialog box.

 The Refresh Rate list includes all settings available for your particular monitor. Using a larger setting causes your monitor to have less flicker, which is an effect that's more visible when the refresh happens less frequently.

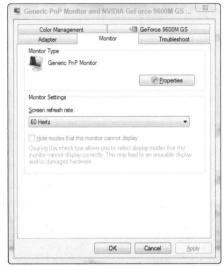

Figure 4-7: The Monitor tab of the Display Settings dialog box

Change the DPI Setting

1. Right-click the desktop and choose Personalize from the resulting menu.

2. In the Control Panel click the Adjust Font Size link on the left of the window.

3. In the DPI Settings dialog box (see Figure 4-8), click the DPI setting you want, or click the Custom DPI button and choose your setting from a drop-down list (see Figure 4-9) and clicking OK to save the setting. Click OK to save any custom DPI settings.

4. Click the Apply button. A message box appears, stating that your new settings will take effect after you restart your computer. Click Restart Now or Restart Later if you don't want to restart the computer at that time.

DPI stands for *dots per inch*. The DPI Setting list includes all DPI settings available for your particular monitor. Using a larger DPI setting (more dots per inch) makes everything you see on your screen larger. Changing your screen resolution has a similar effect.

Figure 4-8: The DPI Settings dialog box

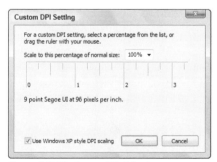

Figure 4-9: The Custom DPI dialog box

Setting Up Input Devices

All the data and images stored on your computer drives are dandy, but unless you can manipulate them, they won't do you much good. That's where input devices come in. You plug input devices into your PC (or, with a wireless device, plug in a USB transmitter) and then use them to add text and images, edit, and generally work with electronic files. You can even use some input devices to play games. You're likely to use a few different types of input devices, so I cover the most common ones in this chapter, including the following:

➡ **Keyboard:** As with typewriters of old, you type on a keyboard to enter text in a document, which might be anything from a word-processed letter or spreadsheet to an e-mail message or a slide presentation. But computer keyboards go further than a typewriter because you can use certain key combinations — called keystroke shortcuts — to take a wide variety of editing and formatting actions such as cutting and pasting objects or text or modifying the appearance of text.

➡ **Mouse:** A mouse is a more tactile kind of input device. Whether it comes in the form of a laptop touchpad you slide your finger around, a mouse you move around your desk, or a mouse with a trackball that you roll with your finger, the basic purpose of a mouse is to move an on-screen cursor that allows you to select objects or text, click and drag objects within a document or between documents, or right-click to display shortcut menus.

➡ **Game controller:** Some models are referred to as joysticks, and some are game pads. Whatever the name or design, the sole purpose of these little guys is to allow you to interact with computer games, moving among space aliens, blitzing bad guys into the ether, and the like.

Get ready to . . .

Identify Different Types of Input Devices

Use this table in tandem with Figure 5-1 and 5-2 to identify different types of input devices.

Device	What It's Used For
Mouse	Select text and objects, double-click to open programs or files, click and drag to move things, quickly scroll through a document, and display shortcut menus
Keyboard	Enter and edit text and numbers, use shortcuts for common actions
Game controller	Maneuver around games, shoot bad guys

 Some PC devices, such as the Tablet PC, also accept input through a touch screen. By using a small, pen-like device called a stylus, you can tap to make selections or write directly on the screen. If you're lucky enough to have one of these fun gadgets, beware: Use only the stylus that came with the device, or you could damage the screen!

 Wireless devices should just about all be Plug and Play these days, which means that Windows Vista can detect and set them up for you as soon as you plug the wireless receiver into a USB port. If the device isn't detected or set up automatically, you may need to install associated software first. See Chapter 19 for information about troubleshooting hardware issues.

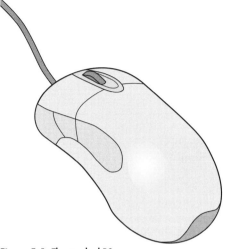

Figure 5-1: The standard PC mouse

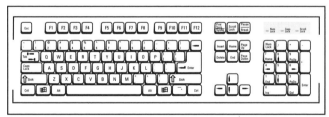

Figure 5-2: An average 104-key keyboard

Customize the Mouse Settings

1. With your mouse plugged into the correct port, it should work with no further settings required on your part. If you'd like to customize the way your mouse works, choose Start⇨Control Panel⇨Hardware and Sound. In the resulting Hardware and Sound window, shown in Figure 5-3, click the Mouse link.

2. In the resulting Mouse Properties dialog box, click the Pointer Options tab, as shown in Figure 5-4. Then do any of the following:

   • Click and drag the Select a Pointer Speed slider to adjust how quickly the mouse cursor moves across your computer screen.

   • Select the Automatically Move Pointer to the Default Button in a Dialog Box check box to enable or disable the Snap To feature.

   • Select the Display Pointer Trails check box to activate this feature and drag the slider to set the cursor trail style; these are essentially shadows that follow your cursor as it moves across the screen. You can choose to hide the cursor while you're typing.

3. Click OK to apply your changes and close the dialog box.

 Use the Buttons tab of the Mouse Properties dialog box to change the functionality of each mouse button. This is especially useful if you're left-handed and would like to switch the functionality of the left and right mouse buttons.

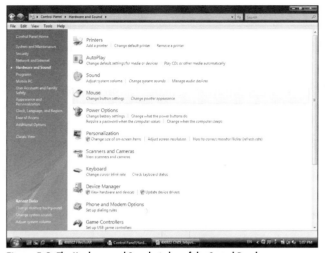

Figure 5-3: The Hardware and Sound window of the Control Panel

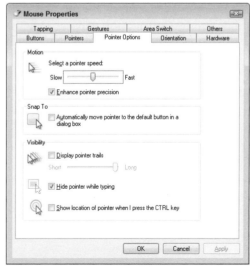

Figure 5-4: The Mouse Properties dialog box

Set Up Your Keyboard

1. Adjusting your keyboard settings might make it easier for you to type, and some of the available settings can be helpful to people with dexterity challenges. To see your options, choose Start⇨Control Panel⇨Hardware and Sound. In the resulting Hardware and Sound window, click the Keyboard link.

2. In the Keyboard Properties dialog box that appears, click the Speed tab (see Figure 5-5) and drag the sliders to adjust the two Character Repeat settings, which do the following:

   - **Repeat Delay:** Affects the amount of time it takes before a typed character is typed again when you hold down a key.

   - **Repeat Rate:** Adjusts how quickly a character repeats when you hold down a key after the first repeat character appears.

3. Drag the slider in the Cursor Blink Rate section. This affects cursors, such as the insertion line that appears in text.

4. Click OK to save and apply changes and close the dialog box.

 If you want to see how the Character Repeat rate settings work in action, click in the text box below the two settings and hold down a key to see a demonstration.

Figure 5-5: The Keyboard Properties dialog box

 If you have trouble with motion (for example, because of arthritis or carpal tunnel syndrome), you might find that you can adjust certain settings to make it easier for you to get your work done. For example, if you can't pick up your finger quickly from a key, a slower repeat rate might save you from typing more instances of a character than you'd intended.

Configure Game Controllers

1. Choose Start⇨Control Panel⇨Hardware and Sound.

2. In the resulting Hardware and Sound window, click the Game Controllers link. (You may have to scroll down to see this link.) The Game Controllers dialog box, as shown in Figure 5-6, appears.

3. In the resulting list of controllers (see Figure 5-7), click the device you want to configure, and then click Properties.

4. On the Test tab of the resulting Properties dialog box move your controller's buttons. The responses in the corresponding areas should match. For example, if you move up the X Axis button on your controller, the + symbol on the X Axis field in the dialog box should move up.

5. If any settings seem inappropriate, you can click the Settings tab and use the Calibrate feature to recalibrate the controller.

6. When you're done testing, click OK to close the dialog box.

 If you're not sure how to modify your device settings, try the Reset to Default button on the Settings tab of the Game Controller Properties dialog box. This resets your device to its factory settings, which in most cases are the most appropriate settings to use.

 Calibrating a game controller helps you to make sure that buttons and features are working correctly. For example, when you recalibrate, you can fine-tune functions such as the sensitivity of your controller to movement and the distance you move a joystick before an action registers.

Figure 5-6: The Game Controller dialog box

Figure 5-7: The list of available game controllers

Setting Up Accessibility Features

Take it from somebody who spends many hours in front of a computer: Customizing the way you interact with Windows pays off by making your computer easier to use as well as decreasing eye or hand strain.

You can set up the way your keyboard and mouse work and turn on accessibility features that help you if you have vision, hearing, or mobility challenges.

To customize Windows Vista for better accessibility, you can do the following:

→ Modify the way the mouse works for left-handed use, change the cursor to sport a certain look, or make the cursor easier to view as it moves around your screen.

→ Work with keyboard settings that make typing and choosing computer commands easier for people who are challenged by physical conditions, such as carpal tunnel syndrome or arthritis.

→ Set up your screen so it's easier to see if you have difficulty reading it.

→ You can even use a Speech Recognition feature that enables the computer to type what you say so you can avoid using a keyboard or mouse (almost) entirely.

→ If you're not sure which features will work for you, you can use an accessibility wizard to let Windows suggest accessibility settings for your particular needs.

Make the Keyboard Easier to Use

1. You can modify your keyboard so it's easier to use if your fingers aren't as nimble as you'd like. To find these settings, choose Start⇨Control Panel⇨Ease of Access and then, in the Ease of Access window that appears (see Figure 6-1), click the Change How Your Keyboard Works link.

2. In the resulting Make the Keyboard Easier to Use window (see Figure 6-2), select any of these settings by selecting a check box:

   • Select the Turn on Mouse Keys check box to control your mouse by keyboard commands. If you turn on this setting, click the Set Up Mouse Keys link to specify settings for this feature. These settings include whether a message or sound notifies you that the feature has been turned on, and the pointer speed that's best for you when controlling mouse functions from your keyboard.

   • Select the Turn on Sticky Keys check box to set up keystroke combinations to be pressed one at a time, rather than in combination. For example, a popular keyboard shortcut is the copy command, which you can perform by pressing the Ctrl key at the same time as you press the C key. Using sticky fingers, you can press first one key and then the other; this might be easier for slow typists or those with hand injuries or arthritis. (See Chapters 10 and 11 for more on copying files and similar commands.)

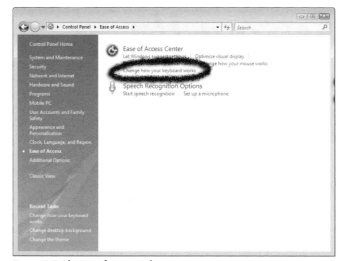

Figure 6-1: The Ease of Access window

 There is setting at the top of the Ease of Access Center that enables features that read the accessibility list to you every time you enter the Center, or scan the section. Scanning the section reads the features to you one after the other until you stop it by turning off the scanning or clicking on a feature to select it.

- If you select the Turn on Toggle Keys check box, Windows Vista plays a sound when you press Caps Lock, Num Lock, or Scroll Lock (which I do all the time by mistake!).

- If you sometimes press a key very lightly by accident or press it so hard it activates twice, you can select the Turn on Filter Keys check box to adjust *repeat rates* (or how rapidly a repeated touch on a key should be taken to invoke a second use of that key rather than a lengthy first press of the key). Use the Set Up Filter Keys link to fine-tune settings in the Set Up Filter Keys dialog box if you make this choice.

- To have Windows Vista underline keyboard shortcuts and *access keys* (you see access keys as underlined letters in menu commands; you can press those letters to choose the command from that menu) wherever these shortcuts appear, select the Underline Keyboard Shortcuts and Access Keys check box (you may have to scroll down to find this option).

3. To save the new settings, click Apply, and then if you're happy with your settings, click the Close button to close the dialog box.

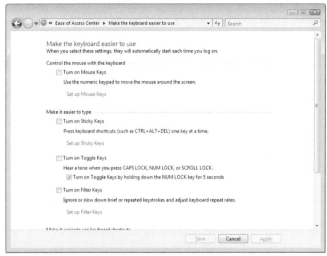

Figure 6-2: The Make the Keyboard Easier to Use window

 Each keyboard has its own unique feel. If your keyboard isn't responsive and you have stiff fingers or a medical condition that makes using the keyboard challenging, you might also try different keyboards to see whether one works better for you than another.

Use the On-Screen Keyboard

1. If you find it easier to click buttons with a mouse than to press keys using your fingers, you might prefer the On-Screen Keyboard. Choose Start⇨Control Panel⇨ Ease of Access to display the Ease of Access window and then click the Ease of Access Center link.

2. In the resulting Ease of Access Center window (see Figure 6-3), click the Start On-Screen Keyboard link. The On-Screen Keyboard appears.

3. Open a document in any application where you can enter text and then click the keys on the On-Screen Keyboard shown in Figure 6-4 to make entries.

4. To change settings, such as how you select keys (Typing Mode) or the font used to label keys (Font), choose Settings and then choose one of four options:

   • Choose **Always on Top** to keep the keyboard on top of applications

   • Choose **Use Click Sound** if you want to hear a plastic "click" whenever you press a key.

   • If you choose the **Typing Mode,** a dialog box appears where you can choose to select objects by hovering over them rather than clicking.

   • If you choose the **Font** option, a dialog box appears allowing you to format the font used when you type with the On-Screen Keyboard. For this and the previous bullet, make settings and then click OK to close the dialog box.

5. Click the Close button to stop using the On-Screen Keyboard.

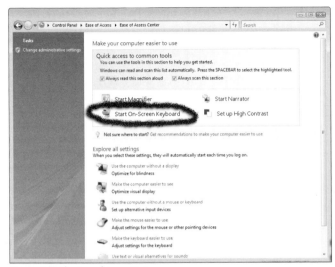

Figure 6-3: The Ease of Access Center

Figure 6-4: The On Screen Keyboard

 To use keystroke combinations (such as Ctrl+Z to undo your last action), click the first key (in this case, Ctrl) and then click the second key (Z). You don't have to hold down the first key as you do with a regular keyboard.

 You can set up the Hover typing mode to activate a key after you place your mouse over it for a predefined period of time (x number of seconds). If you have arthritis or some other condition that makes clicking with your mouse difficult, this option can help you enter text. Choose Settings⇨Typing Mode⇨Hover to Select to activate the Hover mode.

Make the Mouse Easier to Use

1. Choose Start⇨Control Panel⇨Ease of Access to display the Ease of Access window and then click the Change How Your Mouse Works link. The Make the Mouse Easier to Use window opens (see Figure 6-5).

2. Click an item in the Mouse Pointers display to select a different style of mouse pointer.

3. If you want to use the numeric keypad to move your mouse cursor on your screen, select the Turn on Mouse Keys check box. If you turn on this feature, click the Set Up Mouse Keys link to fine-tune its behavior. In the dialog box that appears, adjust settings for keyboard shortcuts to turn this feature on and off, and settings that control the speed with which you can type mouse commands. Click OK to save these settings and return to the Make the Mouse Easier to Use dialog box.

4. Select the Activate a Window by Hovering Over It with the Mouse check box to enable this (pretty self-explanatory!) feature.

5. Click Save to save the new settings.

 You can swap the functionality of the left and right mouse buttons. This can be useful if you're left-handed or if you want to change hands occasionally, which helps you avoid wrist injuries from repetitive motion with one hand. Open the Control Panel and click the Mouse link to display the Mouse Properties dialog box. On the Buttons tab, use the Switch Primary and Secondary Buttons feature to make the right mouse button handle all the usual left button functions, such as clicking and dragging, and the left button handle the typical right-hand functions, such as displaying shortcut menus.

Figure 6-5: The Make the Mouse Easier to Use window

 If you have difficulty seeing the cursor on-screen, experiment with the Windows Vista color scheme, discussed in Chapter 9, to see whether another setting makes your cursor stand out better against the background.

Optimize the Screen for Maximum Visibility

1. Windows Vista has a useful tool that helps improve the visibility of the screen for people who have poor eyesight or who suffer from frequent eyestrain. To see what this feature can do for you, begin by choosing Start⇨Control Panel.

2. In the resulting Control Panel window, click the Optimize Visual Display link under the Ease of Access tools.

3. In the resulting Make the Computer Easier to See window (as shown in Figure 6-6), select the check boxes for features you want to use:

   - **High Contrast:** Make settings for using greater contrast on screen elements.

   - **Hear Text and Descriptions Read Aloud:** You can use these settings to either have the text that appears on your screen read aloud, or hear descriptions of what's happening on your screen (though these are available only with a few selected actions).

Figure 6-6: The Make the Computer Easier to See window

- **Make Things on the Screen Larger:** If you select the Turn on Magnifier check box, you have two cursors on-screen. One cursor appears in the Magnifier window where everything is shown enlarged, and one appears in whatever environment you're working with on your computer (for example, your desktop or an open application). You can maneuver either cursor to work in your document, and the other cursor reflects your move. (They're both active, so it does take some getting used to.)

- **Make Things on the Screen Easier to See:** Here's where you make settings that adjust on-screen contrast to make things easier to see, enlarge the size of the blinking mouse cursor, and get rid of distracting animations and backgrounds. You can also make the rectangle that appears show the movement of a window when you drag it thicker, which can help your eyes track it more easily. (This is called a *focus rectangle.*)

4. When you finish changing settings, click Save to apply them.

 To magnify more of the text, place the mouse cursor at the bottom of the Magnifier window (the mouse cursor changes to a line with an arrow at each end) and drag the cursor down. The size of the Magnifier window increases.

 To close the Magnifier window, press Alt+Tab and select the Magnifier item from the list of open programs. In the Magnifier dialog box, click the Close button.

Set Up Speech Recognition

1. Speech Recognition allows you to speak commands and text into a microphone rather than clicking and typing. You have to set it up to recognize your unique speech inflections and accent. Plug a desktop microphone or headset into your computer (the hole to plug into is typically labeled with a little headphone symbol) and choose Start⇨Control Panel⇨Ease of Access⇨Start Speech Recognition.

2. The Set Up Speech Recognition message appears; click Next to continue. (*Note:* If you've used Speech Recognition before, this message doesn't appear.)

3. In the resulting Set Up Speech Recognition dialog box (as shown in Figure 6-7), select the type of microphone that you're using and then click Next. The next screen tells you how to place and use the microphone for optimum results. Click Next.

4. In the following dialog box (see Figure 6-8), read the sample sentence aloud. When you're done, click Next. If your voice didn't come through loud and clear, the next dialog box asks you to check the microphone connections and try again. If it did come through you see the Microphone Is Now Set Up window. Click Next to proceed.

 During the Speech Recognition setup procedure, you're given the option of printing out commonly used commands. It's a good idea to do this because speech commands aren't always second nature!

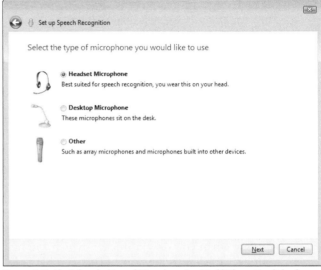

Figure 6-7: The Select the Type of Microphone You Would Like to Use dialog box

5. In the resulting dialog box, choose whether to enable or disable document view. Document view allows Windows Vista to review your documents and e-mail to help it recognize your speech patterns. After you've made your choice, click Next.

6. In the resulting dialog box, if you want to view and/or print a list of speech recognition commands, click the View Reference Sheet button, and then click the Close button to close that window. Click Next to proceed.

7. In the resulting dialog box, either deselect the Run Speech Recognition at Startup check box to disable this feature or leave the default setting. Click Next. The final dialog box informs you that you can now control the computer by voice, and it offers you a Start Tutorial button to help you practice voice commands. Click that button to start the tutorial or click Cancel to skip the tutorial and leave the Speech Recognition setup.

8. The Speech Recognition control panel appears (see Figure 6-9). Say, "Start listening" to activate the feature and begin using spoken commands to work with your computer.

 To stop Speech Recognition, click the Close button on the Speech Recognition control panel window. To start the Speech Recognition feature again, choose Start⇨Control Panel⇨Ease of Access and then click the Start Speech Recognition link. To find out more about Speech Recognition commands, click the Speech Recognition Options link in the Ease of Access window and then click the Take Speech Tutorials link in the Speech Recognition Options window.

Figure 6-8: The Adjust the Microphone Volume dialog box

Figure 6-9: The Speech Recognition control panel

Replace Sounds with Visual Cues

1. Windows plays sounds to signify some events, such as the appearance of a warning message or the closing of a program. If you're hard of hearing and want an alternative way for Windows to notify you of these events, you can change your computer settings to give you visual clues. To access these settings, choose Start⇨Control Panel⇨Ease of Access.

2. Click the Replace Sounds with Visual Cues link.

3. In the resulting Use Text or Visual Alternatives for Sounds window (see Figure 6-10), adjust any of the following settings:

   - If you select the Turn on Visual Notifications for Sounds (Sound Sentry) check box, Windows Vista will play sounds along with a display of visual cues.

   - Select a setting for visual warnings. These warnings essentially flash a portion of your screen to alert you to an event.

   - To have Windows display text captions whenever a sound occurs, select the Turn on Text Captions for Spoken Dialog (When Available) check box.

4. To save the new settings, click Save.

 This might seem obvious, but if you're hard of hearing, you might want to simply increase the volume for your speakers. You can do this by using the volume adjustment in a program such as Windows Media Player (see Chapter 13). Alternatively, you can modify your system volume by choosing Hardware and Sound in the Control Panel and then clicking the Adjust System Volume Click and drag the slider controls in the resulting dialog box to adjust the volume.

Figure 6-10: The Use Text or Visual Alternatives for Sounds window

 Visual cues are useful if you're hard of hearing and don't always pick up system sounds alerting you to error messages or a device disconnect. After the setting is turned on, it's active until you go back to the Use Text or Visual Alternatives for Sounds dialog box and turn it off.

Let Windows Suggest Accessibility Settings

1. Windows can suggest the best settings for you based on a series of answers you provide to questions about your vision, hearing, or hand dexterity. Choose Start⇨ Control Panel.

2. Click the Let Windows Suggest Settings link.

3. In the resulting Get Recommendations to Make Your Computer Easier to Use dialog box (see Figure 6-11), click in any checkbox that applies to your vision and then click Next.

4. Continue to select appropriate checkboxes in the following dialog boxes: Dexterity, Hearing, Speech, and Reasoning, and then click Done.

5. In the resulting Recommended Settings dialog box (see Figure 6-12), select the checkbox for any setting you wish to turn on. Click the Apply button to activate selected features.

6. Click the Close button to close the dialog box.

 Not every accessibility feature in the world is built into Windows Vista. To find others, scroll to the bottom of the Recommended Settings dialog box and click the Learn about Additional Assistive Technologies Online link to view assistive technologies you can purchase from third parties in the Windows Marketplace.

Figure 6-11: Get Recommendations to Make Your Computer Easier to Use dialog box

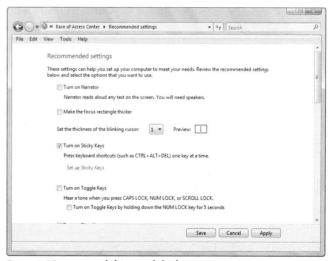

Figure 6-12: Recommended Settings dialog box

Part II
Getting to Know Windows

The 5th Wave   By Rich Tennant

"The funny thing is he's spent 9 hours organizing his computer desktop."

Adjusting Windows Settings

*W*indows includes several settings that you can use to keep your data safe, enable different users to have accounts on your computer, or control your computer clock. You can also set up how Windows software receives updates that may help keep your computer secure.

In this chapter, you discover how to make the following settings:

➡ **You can set up a password** that you have to enter when you want to use Windows. Setting up a password keeps others from accessing your data, which includes not only files on your computer, but also any browser settings you've made to save passwords for online accounts.

➡ You can create several **Windows user accounts** on your computer. When you create a user account several settings and files for that user are kept unique from other users.

➡ Your computer **date and time** feature can be modified to reflect your current location. If you use a laptop or move to a new location you might want to modify your date and time settings so Windows runs automated features at the time you want and features such as inserting a date in a word processed program work accurately.

➡ **Windows Update** is a tool you can use to make sure your computer has the most up-to-date files and security measures in place. When a new operating system like Windows Vista is released, it has been thoroughly tested; however, when the product is in general use, the manufacturer begins to find a few problems or security gaps that it couldn't anticipate. For that reason, companies such as Microsoft release updates to their software, both to fix those problems and deal with new threats to computers that appeared after the software release. You can install these automatically or manually.

Get ready to . . .

Set Up a Windows Password

1. You can assign a password to any account to keep others from being able to log on without your permission. Choose Start⇨Control Panel⇨User Accounts and Family Safety.

2. In the resulting window, click the Change Your Windows Password link. Then, if you have more than one user account, click the account you want to add the password to. Click the Create a Password for Your Account link, shown in Figure 7-1.

3. In the Create a Password for Your Account screen, shown in Figure 7-2, enter a password, confirm it, and add a password hint.

4. Click the Create Password button. Note if you have previously set a password this button will be labeled Change Password.

5. You see the Make Changes to Your User Account window again. If you want to remove your password at some point, you can click the Remove Your Password link.

6. Click the Close button to close the User Accounts window.

 Anybody can change the password for his or her own account, but only an account with administrator privileges can change passwords for others' accounts.

 After you create a password, you can go to the User Accounts and Family Safety window and change it at any time by clicking the Change Your Windows Password link. You can also change the name on your user account by clicking the Change Your Account Name link in the User Accounts and Family Safety window.

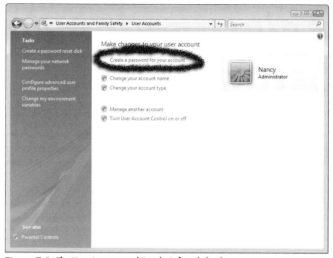

Figure 7-1: The User Accounts and Family Safety dialog box

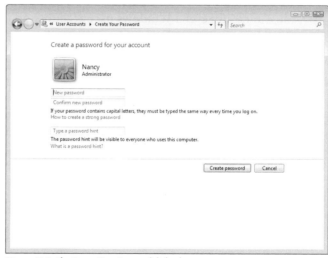

Figure 7-2: The Create Your Password dialog box

Set Up Additional User Accounts

1. When you set up your computer, you create your user account. If you want to create additional accounts make sure your account has administrator privileges and then you can follow these steps. Choose Start⇨Control Panel.

2. In the resulting Control Panel window, click the Add or Remove User Accounts link.

3. In the resulting Manage Accounts window, shown in Figure 7-3, click the Create a New Account link.

4. In the Manage Accounts window that appears, shown in Figure 7-4, enter an account name and then select the type of account you want to create:

   • **Standard User,** who can't do the tasks an administrator can.

   • **Administrator,** who can do things like create and change accounts and install programs. Typically, it's a good idea to allow only one person to have administrator privileges to avoid confusion.

5. Click the Create Account button and then close the Control Panel.

 After you create an account, you can make changes to it, such as assigning a password or changing the account type, by double-clicking it in the Manage Accounts window you reached in Step 4 of the preceding step list and following the links listed there.

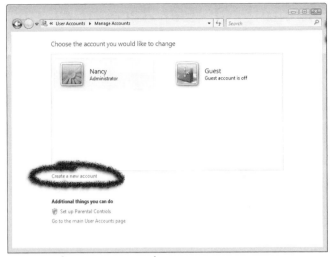

Figure 7-3: The Manage Accounts window

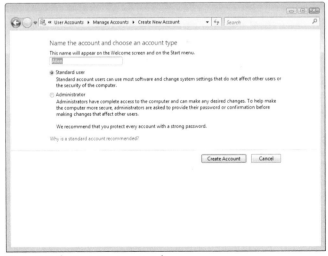

Figure 7-4: The Create New Account window

Change Your User Account Picture

1. If you don't like the picture associated with your user account, you can change it. Choose Start⇨Control Panel⇨Add or Remove User Accounts.

2. In the resulting Manage Accounts window, shown in Figure 7-5, click the account you want to change.

3. Click the Change Your Picture link and in the resulting window, shown in Figure 7-6, click another picture (or browse to see more picture choices) to select it.

4. Click the Change Picture button; the dialog box closes.

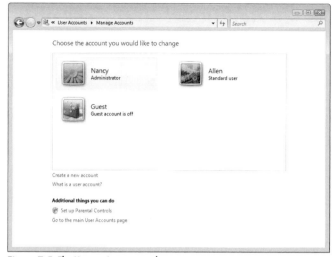

Figure 7-5: The Manage Accounts window

Figure 7-6: The Change Your Picture window

Set the Date and Time

1. The date and clock on your computer keep good time, but you might have to provide the correct date and time for your location. To get started, press the Windows key on your keyboard to display the taskbar if it isn't visible.

2. Right-click the Date/Time display on the far right of the taskbar and then choose Adjust Date/Time from the shortcut menu that appears.

3. In the Date and Time dialog box that appears (see Figure 7-7), click the Change Date and Time button.

4. In the Date and Time Settings dialog box that appears (see Figure 7-8), click a new date in the Date calendar. Enter a new time in the Time text box to change the time or use the spinner arrows to choose a different time.

5. Click OK twice to apply the new settings and close the dialog boxes.

 If you don't want your computer to adjust for Daylight Saving Time, click the Change Time Zone button and deselect the Automatically Adjust Clock for Daylight Saving Time check box to turn off this feature.

 Another option for displaying the time or date is to add the Clock or Calendar gadget to the Windows Sidebar. You can also drag gadgets right onto your desktop if you prefer not to leave the Sidebar displayed. See Chapter 5 for more about using the Sidebar and gadgets.

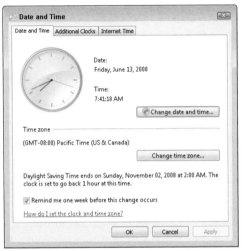

Figure 7-7: The Date and Time dialog box

Figure 7-8: The Date and Time Settings dialog box

Set Up Windows Update to Run Automatically

1. You can set Windows Update to work in a few different ways by choosing Start⇨All Programs⇨Windows Update and clicking the Change Settings link on the left side of the Windows Update window that appears.

2. In the resulting window (see Figure 7-9), you find these settings:

   • **Install Updates Automatically:** With this setting, Windows Update starts at a time of day you specify, but your computer must be on for it to work. If you've turned off your computer, the automatic update will start when you next turn on your computer, and it might shut down your computer in the middle of your work to complete the installation.

   • **Download Updates But Let Me Choose Whether to Install Them:** You can set up Windows Update to download updates and have Windows notify you (through a little pop-up message on your taskbar) when they're available, but you get to decide when the updates are installed and when your computer reboots (turns off and then on) to complete the installation. This is my preferred setting because I have control and won't be caught unaware by a computer reboot.

   • **Check for Updates But Let Me Choose Whether to Download and Install Them:** With this setting, you neither download nor install updates until you say so, but Windows notifies you that new updates are available.

   • **Never Check for Updates:** You can stop Windows from checking for updates and check for them your-

self, manually (see the following task). This puts your computer at a bit more risk, but it's useful for you to know how to perform a manual update if you discover a new update is available that you need to proceed with a task (such as getting updated drivers or a language pack).

3. Click Install Updates Automatically and click the Day and Time boxes and select a day and time when the update should run.

4. Click OK to close the dialog box and save the new settings.

 Windows updates are helpful in keeping your computer secure, because many updates address newly found security gaps in the operating system. See Chapter 20 for more about Windows security features and settings.

Figure 7-9: The Windows Update Change Settings window

Run Windows Update

1. No matter which Windows Update setting you choose (see the preceding task) you can run a manual update at any time. To do so, choose Start⇨All Programs⇨ Windows Update.

2. In the resulting Windows Update window, click Check for Updates. Windows thinks about this for a while, so feel free to page through a magazine for a minute or two.

3. In the resulting window, as shown in Figure 7-10, click the View Available Updates link.

4. In the following window, which shows the available updates (see Figure 7-11), select check boxes for the updates that you want to install. (It usually doesn't hurt to just accept all updates, if you have the time to download them all). Then click the Install button.

5. A window appears, showing the progress of your installation. When the installation is complete, you might get a message telling you that it's a good idea to restart your computer to complete the installation. Click the Restart Now button.

 You can set up Windows Update to run at the same time every day. Click the Change Settings link in the left pane of the Windows Update window and choose the frequency (such as every day) and time of day to check for and install updates.

 If you set Windows Update to run automatically, be forewarned that when it runs it might also automatically restart your computer to finish the update installation sequence. Although it displays a pop-up message warning that it's about to do this, it's easy to miss. Then you might be startled to find that whatever you're working on shuts down and your computer restarts when you least expect it.

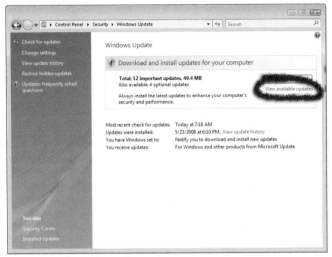

Figure 7-10: The Windows Update window

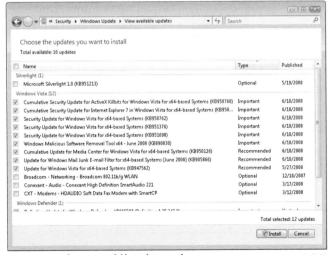

Figure 7-11: The View Available Updates window

Getting Around the Windows Desktop

*J*ust as your desk is the central area from which you do all kinds of work, the Windows Vista desktop is a command center for organizing your computer work. The desktop appears when you log on to a Windows Vista computer. The Start menu is located on the desktop; you use this menu to access your computer settings, files, folders, and software. On the desktop there is also a taskbar that offers settings, such as your computer's date and time, as well as shortcuts to your most frequently accessed programs or files.

This chapter is an introduction to all the things you can do via the desktop. Along the way, you discover the Recycle Bin, where you place deleted files and folders, and the Quick Launch bar, which allows quick access to commonly used programs. You also find out how to work with application windows, create a desktop shortcut, and get help.

Chapter

8

Get ready to . . .

Customize the Quick Launch Bar

1. The Quick Launch bar can be a handy tool for starting programs, and you can customize it to contain the programs you use most often. Locate the Quick Launch bar on the taskbar just to the right of the Start button; if it's not visible, right-click the taskbar and choose Toolbars⇨Quick Launch from the shortcut menu (see Figure 8-1).

2. To place any application on the Quick Launch bar, right-click that application in the Start menu or on the Desktop (as shown in Figure 8-2) and then choose Add to Quick Launch. You can also click an icon, and while keeping the mouse button pressed, drag that icon to the Quick Launch bar.

If you have more programs in this area than can be shown on the taskbar, click the arrows to the right of the Quick Launch bar; a shortcut menu of programs appears. However, don't create too much clutter on your Quick Launch bar; if you do, it can become unwieldy. Logical candidates to place here are your Internet browser, your e-mail program, and programs that you use every day, such as a word processor or calendar program.

When the Quick Launch bar is displayed, the Show Desktop button is available. When you click this button, all open applications are reduced to taskbar icons. It's a quick way to view your desktop — or hide what you're up to!

Figure 8-1: Displaying the Quick Launch bar

Figure 8-2: Adding programs to the Quick Launch bar

Arrange Icons on the Desktop

1. To avoid icon clutter, you can sort the shortcut icons on your desktop in neat rows based on a criterion, such as the most recently used to the least recently used. First, right-click the desktop and choose View in the resulting shortcut menu; be sure that Auto Arrange isn't selected, as shown in Figure 8-3. (If it is selected, deselect it before proceeding to the next step.)

2. Right-click the Windows Vista desktop. In the resulting shortcut menu, choose Sort By and then choose the criterion for sorting your desktop icons (see Figure 8-4). For example, you can arrange them alphabetically by name or from smallest file to the largest file.

3. You can also click any desktop icon and drag it to another location on the desktop — for example, to separate it from other desktop icons so you can find it easily.

 If you've sorted or manually rearranged your desktop by moving items hither, thither, and yon and you want to instantly move your icons into orderly rows along the left side of your desktop, snap them into place with the Auto Arrange feature. Right-click the desktop and then choose View⇨Auto Arrange.

Figure 8-3: Deselecting AutoArrange

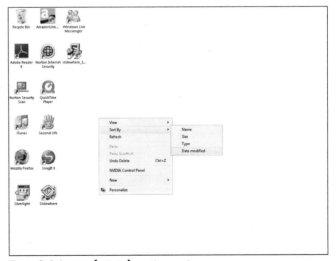

Figure 8-4: A menu of criteria for sorting your icons

Create a Desktop Shortcut

1. Shortcuts are a useful way to quickly access items you use on a frequent basis. To create a new shortcut, first choose Start⇨All Programs and locate the program on the menu that appears.

2. Right-click an item — FreeCell, for example — and choose Send To⇨Desktop (Create Shortcut), as shown in Figure 8-5.

3. The shortcut appears on the desktop (see Figure 8-6). Double-click the shortcut icon to open the application.

 You can create a shortcut for items other than applications by right-clicking the desktop, choosing New, and then choosing an item to place there, such as a text document, bitmap image, or contact. Then double-click the shortcut that appears and begin working on the file in the associated application.

 Occasionally, Windows Vista offers to delete desktop icons that you haven't used in a long time. Let it. The desktop should be reserved for frequently used programs, files, and folders. You can always re-create shortcuts easily if you need them again. To clean up your desktop manually, right-click the desktop and choose Personalize. In the Personalization window that appears, click the Change Desktop Icons link in the Tasks list on the left. In the Desktop Icons setting dialog box that appears, click the Restore Default button, which restores the original desktop shortcuts that were set up on your computer.

Figure 8-5: Using the Send To command to create a shortcut

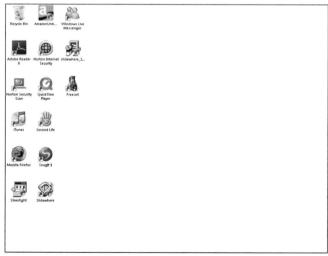

Figure 8-6: Shortcut icons on the desktop

Empty the Recycle Bin

1. Files that you place in the Windows Recycle Bin stay there until you empty it or until it reaches its size limit and Windows dumps a few files. To empty the trash yourself, right-click the Recycle Bin icon on the Windows Vista desktop and choose Empty Recycle Bin from the shortcut menu that appears (see Figure 8-7).

2. In the confirmation dialog box that appears, click Yes to confirm that you want to delete the items. A progress dialog box appears indicating the contents are being deleted. Remember that after you empty the Recycle Bin, all files previously in it are unavailable to you. Chapter 10 has more details about deleting files.

 Up until the moment you permanently delete items by performing the preceding steps or until Windows deletes files because the Recycle Bin has reached its capacity, you can retrieve items in the Recycle Bin. Start by right-clicking the desktop icon and choosing Open. Select the item you want to retrieve and then click the Restore This Item link near the top of the Recycle Bin window.

 You can modify the Recycle Bin properties by right-clicking it and choosing Properties. In the dialog box that appears, you can change the maximum size for the Recycle Bin and change where it should be stored on your hard drive. You can also deselect the option of having a confirmation dialog box appear when you delete Recycle Bin contents.

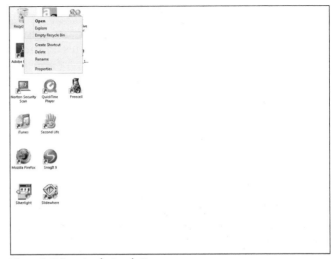

Figure 8-7: Emptying the Recycle Bin

Set Up Windows Vista Sidebar

1. To get started with the Sidebar and the useful gadgets that it holds, choose Start➪Control Panel➪Appearance and Personalization. Choose whether to Keep Sidebar on Top of Other Windows (in the Windows Sidebar Properties category) to open the Windows Sidebar Properties dialog box.

2. Select the Start Sidebar When Windows Starts option to ensure that the Sidebar always displays when you start your computer.

3. If you want to, select the Sidebar Is Always on Top of Other Windows check box if you want other applications to be behind the Sidebar.

4. Click OK and then click the Close button to close the Control Panel window. The Sidebar appears, as shown in Figure 8-8. (Note that you can also click the Sidebar icon on the Windows Notification Area to instantly display the Sidebar at any time).

> If you're left-handed or have some other propensity for things on the left, you can choose to have the Sidebar displayed on the left side of the screen by selecting the Left radio button in the Windows Sidebar Properties dialog box.

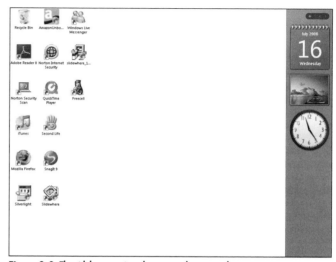

Figure 8-8: The sidebar contains whatever gadgets you place on it

5. Click a displayed gadget and drag it to the desktop if you want it to stay there even after the Sidebar is closed.

6. To display more gadgets, click the Gadgets symbol (a plus sign) at the top of the Sidebar.

7. In the resulting Add Gadgets dialog box (see Figure 8-9), double-click a gadget (or click and drag it to the Sidebar). If you need to view additional gadgets, click the Get More Gadgets Online link in the lower-right corner of the dialog box.

8. Click the Close button to close the dialog box.

 If you display gadgets and then click and drag them onto the desktop, even if you close the Sidebar, they stay visible. So if you want to save desktop space, find the gadgets you like, plop them on your desktop, and hide the Sidebar!

Figure 8-9: The Add Gadgets dialog box

Resize a Window

1. You can make application windows bigger or smaller to focus on the one you're working in or to see more than one at a time. One way to resize windows is to click the Restore Down button (the icon showing two overlapping windows) in the top-right corner of a program window. The window reduces in size.

2. To enlarge a window that has been restored down to again fill the screen, click the Maximize button (see Figure 8-10). (**Note:** This button is in the same location as the Restore Down button; this button toggles to one or the other, depending on whether you have the screen reduced in size or maximized. A ScreenTip identifies the button when you pass your mouse over it.)

3. To size a window more precisely, click and drag any corner of a reduced window. By doing this, you can resize it manually.

 With a window maximized, you can't move the window. If you reduce a window in size, you can then click and hold the title bar to drag the window around the desktop, which is one way to view more than one window on your screen at the same time.

Figure 8-10: Toggle between Maximize and Restore Down

Customize the Start Menu

1. Press the Windows key on your keyboard to display the Start menu. Right-click anywhere on an empty part of the Start menu and choose Properties.

2. In the resulting Taskbar and Start Menu Properties dialog box, click the Customize button to display the Customize Start Menu dialog box, as shown in Figure 8-11. You can do the following:

    -   Click to set standard or large icon size.

    -   Click the up or down arrows on the Number of Programs on Start Menu text box to display more or fewer of your frequently used programs.

    -   Use the lists of alternate Internet and e-mail programs to select different applications to appear on the Start menu.

3. Scroll down the list of computer features and use the radio buttons to select how features, such as Search (see Figure 8-12) will work.

4. After you finish making selections, click OK to save the new settings. Your Start menu reflects your changes, showing items for accessing and running programs and features.

 Right-click the list of programs in the Start menu and choose Sort By Name to alphabetize the list. Folders get reordered to appear first, followed by individual programs.

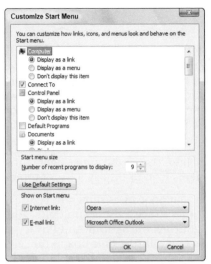

Figure 8-11: The Customize Start Menu dialog box

Figure 8-12: Settings for Windows Search

Get Help

1. You can browse Help by topic. Choose Start↪Help and Support to open the Windows Help and Support window. *Note:* If your copy of Windows came built into your computer, some computer manufacturers (such as Hewlett-Packard) customize this center to add information that's specific to your computer system, making it slightly different than my instructions here indicate.

2. Click the Browse Help icon in the upper-right corner or the Table of Contents icon to display a list of topics.

3. In the new screen that appears as shown in Figure 8-13, click any of the topics to see a list of subtopics. For example, you might click the Security and Privacy topic, then on Windows Firewall (the blue box to the left of that topic tells you there are additional subtopics here) and then click Using Windows Firewall. Eventually, you get down to the deepest level of detailed subtopics (in this example, a subtopic article would be Turn Windows Firewall On and Off); these have question mark icons next to them, as shown in Figure 8-14.

4. Click a subtopic to read its contents. Some subtopics contain blue links that lead to related topics. Links with a green arrow next to them perform an action when clicked, such as opening a dialog box so you can complete a task.

5. Click any word in green to view a definition of that term. Click outside the definition to close it.

6. When you finish reading a help topic, click the Close button to close the Help and Support window.

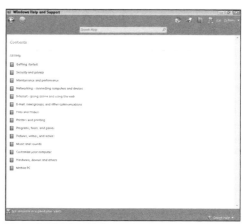

Figure 8-13: A list of help topics

Figure 8-14: Drill down through topics and subtopics to find info

Search Help

1. If you don't find what you need by using the Table of Contents (for instance, say you wanted help using your mouse but didn't realize that's listed under the topic Getting Started), you might want to use the help search feature to find what you need by entering keywords such as *mouse* or *input*. Choose Start⇨Help and Support to open the Help and Support window.

2. Enter a search term (such as *"input devices"*) in the Search Help text box and then click the Search Help button (the little magnifying glass icon on the right of the search box). The top search results, such as those shown in Figure 8-15, appear.

3. Click one of the numbered results to view a detailed article. Use the links listed under In This Article to jump to a section of the article that's of interest.

4. In some cases, these articles have links to other topics or subtopics (see Figure 8-16). Click any link under the See Also list at the bottom of the topic or a link within the article to go to related topics.

5. If the subtopic doesn't do the trick, click the Back arrow in the top-left corner to go back to the list of search results and click another one. If you still have no luck, try entering a different search term in the Search text box and clicking Search Help again.

 If you don't find what you need with Search, consider clicking the Browse Help button (the icon that looks like a little blue book) in the top-right corner of the Windows Help and Support window to display a list of major topics. The topics might also give you some ideas for good search terms to continue your search.

Figure 8-15: Top search results

Figure 8-16: An article with links to more articles

Connect to Remote Assistance

1. Remote Assistance allows you to permit somebody else to view or take control of your computer using the Internet to help fix a problem. Be aware that by doing so you give the person access to all your files, so be sure this is somebody you trust. To use Remote Assistance, you and the other person have to have Windows Vista and an Internet connection.

2. First enable Remote Assistance by choosing Start↔ Control Panel↔System and Maintenance ↔ Allow Remote Access.

3. On the Remote tab of the resulting Systems Properties dialog box, as shown in Figure 8-17, select the Allow Remote Assistance Connections to This Computer check box and then click OK.

4. Choose Start↔Help and Support to open the Help and Support window. Click the Windows Remote Assistance link in the Ask Someone area.

5. In the resulting Windows Remote Assistance dialog box, as shown in Figure 8-18, click the Invite Someone You Trust to Help You link.

6. On the page that appears, choose an e-mail method to notify somebody that you want help depending on whether you have e-mail set up on your computer or not. You can find more details about using e-mail in Chapter 17. Assuming you have e-mail set up, click Save this Invitation as a File.

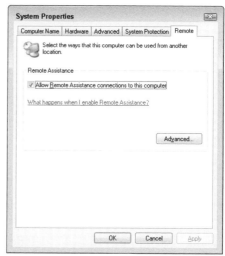

Figure 8-17: Getting help from others by using remote assistance

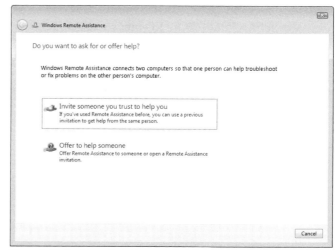

Figure 8-18: Sending an invitation to ask for help

7. Enter and retype a password which your helper must enter to access your computer and click Finish. (The password must be at least six characters long.)

8. Your default e-mail program opens with an invitation message prepared. Fill in your helper's e-mail address in the To field. (The address will look something like Chris@yahoo.com, with the @ sign and the period separating the different parts of the address.) If you like, add a personal message at the end of the automatically generated invitation. (However for security reasons, it's better to call the person to give him the password than to put a password in the e-mail message.) Click Send.

9. The Windows Remote Assistance window appears, as shown in Figure 8-19, and it awaits an external connection; your remote helper now can connect and view and navigate around your computer in a window on his or her own computer. When an incoming connection is made, you and your helper can use the tools here to do the following:

   • **Chat:** Use this feature to enter messages and chat via text with your helper; if you prefer, you can just get on the phone with the person to have a live conversation.

   • **Send file:** You might want to send a file, for example, if you're having trouble opening a file and want your helper to see whether it's corrupted, or if you downloaded a help article that you think your helper should read.

   • **Pause, cancel, or stop sharing:** At any time, you can pause your sharing to take away access to your computer, cancel the session entirely, or just stop sharing with that individual.

10. When you're finished, click the Close button to close the Windows Remote Assistance window.

Figure 8-19: The Windows Remote Assistance window

 Remember that it's up to you to let the recipient know the password — it isn't included in your e-mail unless you add it (which I advise against because e-mail isn't secure). Although using a password used to be optional in Windows XP, it's mandatory in Windows Vista.

Customize the Look of Windows

Chapter

9

ake it from somebody who spends many hours in front of a computer: Customizing the way Windows looks and feels pays off by making your computer easier to use as well as decreasing eyestrain. In addition, you get a computer that looks the way you want it to.

To customize how Windows Vista appears, you can do the following:

➡ Change the desktop background to show different colors or images. You can even pick a preset theme that combines a color scheme and desktop background image in pleasing combinations.

➡ Set up the sharpness with which Windows Vista displays images and colors.

➡ Use screen saver settings to display the photo from your bike trip through France or an interesting animation. You can set a screen saver to appear when you stop using your computer for a certain period of time, which is useful to keep whatever project you're working on private.

➡ Change the color scheme Windows uses for various on-screen elements.

Get ready to . . .

Set Up Your Screen Resolution

1. Right-click the desktop to display a shortcut menu and then choose Personalize.

2. In the resulting Personalization window, click the Display Settings link.

3. In the Display Settings dialog box that appears (as shown in Figure 9-1), move the Resolution slider to a higher or lower resolution. You can also choose how many colors your computer uses for display by making a choice in the Colors drop-down list.

4. Click OK to accept the new screen resolution.

 Higher resolutions, such as 1400 x 1250, produce smaller, crisper images. Lower resolutions, such as 800 x 600, produce larger, somewhat jagged images. The upside of higher resolution is that more fits on your screen; the downside is that words and graphics can be too small to see easily.

 The Colors setting of the Display Properties dialog box offers two settings. The lower color quality is 16-bit; the highest is 32-bit. Essentially, the higher the bits, the more color definition you get.

 Remember that you can also use your View settings in most software programs to get a larger or smaller view of your documents without having to change your screen's resolution. Most applications provide a View menu; click it to access commands such as Zoom. Microsoft Office products have not only a View menu, but an easy to use zoom slider in the bottom right corner you can use to instantly shrink or enlarge a document on screen.

Figure 9-1: Use the slider to change the resolution

Choose a Desktop Theme

1. To apply a predesigned theme that controls your desktop appearance, first right-click the desktop and choose Personalize. The Personalization window opens. Click the Theme link.

2. In the resulting Theme Settings dialog box, shown in Figure 9-2, select a theme from the Theme drop-down list. You have the following options:

   • **Windows Vista** offers up a beautiful lake and mountains against a blue sky. The color scheme that this theme uses for various on-screen elements, such as window title bars, relies heavily on grays, blues, and reds.

   • **Windows Classic** sports a plain blue background with silvery-blue and gray colors for screen elements.

   • **My Current Theme** uses whatever settings you have and saves them with that name.

   • **Browse** takes you to the Program Files folder of Windows, where you can look for any files with the .theme extension. It's not that Windows Vista comes with a lot of these waiting in this folder for you to use, but if you like, you can buy themes from third-party companies at sites such as www.my vistathemes.com and www.vista-themes. net.

3. Click OK to apply the selected theme.

Figure 9-2: Choosing a theme in the Theme Settings dialog box

 If you apply a theme and then make changes to your colors or background, you can save it as a custom theme. Just click the Save As button in the Theme Settings dialog box discussed in the step above to keep your new theme for future use.

Change the Desktop Background

1. The desktop background can consist of a solid color or a photo or graphical image. Right-click the desktop and choose Personalize from the shortcut menu.

2. In the resulting Personalization window, click the Desktop Background link to display the Desktop Background window, as shown in Figure 9-3.

3. Select a category of desktop background options from the Location drop-down list to display previews of certain types of images:

   • **Windows Wallpapers** are photos and graphical backgrounds Microsoft has built into Windows Vista.

   • **Pictures** opens your Pictures folder, allowing you to use one of your own images as your desktop background. In Figure 9-4, I've chosen a photo as a background.

   • **Sample Pictures** allows you to choose from samples included in your Sample Pictures folder, which is located in your Pictures folder.

   • **Public Pictures** allows you to browse to locate any image on your computer or computer network in the Public folder.

   • **Solid Colors** allows you to choose from a palette of preselected colors.

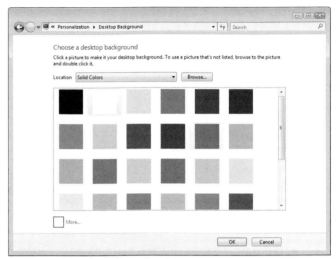

Figure 9-3: The Display Background window

 Try uploading pictures from your digital camera into your Pictures folder. You can then use the procedure described here to make any photo your desktop background. You can also download free images from the Internet to your Pictures folder and use them in the same way.

4. Click the image you want to use. The background is previewed on your desktop.

5. If you select an option other than Solid Colors, you can also control whether one large image or several smaller images appear and whether the image is centered. From the positioning options at the bottom of the dialog box, select one of the following:

   - **Fit to Screen:** This option stretches one copy of the image to fill the screen, covering any background color completely.

   - **Tile:** This choice displays multiple copies of the image filling the desktop. The number of images depends on the size and resolution of the original graphic.

   - **Center:** Quite logically, this option centers the image on a colored background so that you can see a solid border around its edges. The background photo in Figure 9-4 is centered.

6. Click OK to apply the settings and close the dialog box.

Figure 9-4: A centered photo serves as the desktop background

 If you apply a desktop theme (see more about this in the previous task), you overwrite whatever desktop settings you've made in this task. If you apply a desktop theme and then go back and make desktop settings, you replace the theme's settings. However, making changes is easy and keeps your desktop interesting, so play around with themes and desktop backgrounds all you like!

Set Up a Screen Saver

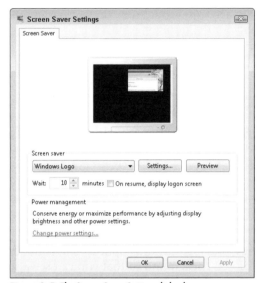

1. If you choose to use a screen saver, you can set how long your computer is inactive before that screen saver appears. Right-click the desktop and choose Personalize. In the resulting Personalization window, click the Screen Saver link to display the Screen Saver Settings dialog box (see Figure 9-5).

2. Click the downward-pointing triangle to open the Screen Saver drop-down list and then choose a screen saver from the list. If you want to use the photos in your own Picture folder, choose the Photos option. Other choices are a mixture of purely graphical animations and short movies such as Nature; just pick the one that appeals to you.

3. Use the arrows in the Wait *xx* Minutes text box to set the number of inactivity minutes that Windows Vista waits before displaying the screen saver.

4. Click the Preview button to take a peek at your screen saver of choice (see Figure 9-6). The new selection previews in a full screen view for a few moments and then disappears and continues to preview in the small screen window in the dialog box.

5. When you're happy with your settings, click OK.

 If you decide that you don't want a screen saver to appear, choose None from the Screen Saver drop-down list in the Screen Saver Settings dialog box.

Figure 9-5: The Screen Saver Settings dialog box

Figure 9-6: Previewing your screen saver

Change Your Color Scheme

1. Right-click the desktop and choose Personalize.

2. In the resulting Personalization window, click the Window Color and Appearance link to display the Appearance Settings dialog box (see Figure 9-7).

3. Click a color scheme and make settings for transparency and color intensity.

4. To customize the selected preset color scheme, click the Advanced button.

5. In the resulting Advanced Appearance dialog box, as shown in Figure 9-8, select a screen element from the Item drop-down list and then adjust settings for size, color, font, or effects such as bold; repeat this for each screen element you want to change.

6. Click OK to close the Advanced Appearance dialog box and apply all changes.

 If you want to set specific colors in the Advanced Appearance dialog box and you know the Red/Green/Blue value for those colors, in the Color drop-down lists click Other and enter specific values for Red, Green, and Blue. Click OK to save the changes.

 Some colors are easier on the eyes than others. For example, green is more restful to look at than orange. Choose a color scheme that's pleasant to look at and easy on the eyes!

Figure 9-7: Selecting a color scheme

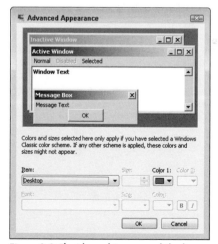

Figure 9-8: The Advanced Appearance dialog box

Manage Control Panel Appearance

1. Windows Vista allows you to change your Control Panel options to look like earlier versions of Windows. If you feel comfortable with a previous version's look and feel choose Start⇨Control Panel.

2. In the result Control Panel window (see Figure 9-9) click the Classic View link on the left. The panel changes to the classic look (see Figure 9-10).

3. To return to the Windows Visa Control Panel click the Control Panel Home link on the left.

 To use the Windows Vista Control Panel settings you click on various links; major categories typically have subcategory links so you can jump more directly to what you need. The Classic View offers individual icons for tasks rather than hierarchal links. You can double-click any of those icons to move to the next step, which is often a dialog box you can use to make settings.

Figure 9-9: Windows Vista Control Panel

Figure 9-10: Windows Classic View

Part III
Getting to Work

The 5th Wave By Rich Tennant

Working with Files and Folders

Chapter 10

*P*eople have been using folders to store paperwork for years. When computers came into common use, some clever person adopted this model for the way that a computer stores. *Files* are the individual documents that you create and save from within applications, such as Word and Excel. When you save a computer file, you can store it in a folder to organize your work logically. You can create folders and even subfolders and give them names, such as Household Inventory or Vacation Plans, to organize your files by project or topic.

You can also move files and folders around after you create them if you find you need to reorganize them, just as you might shuffle papers to different folders in the real world.

In this chapter, you find out how to organize and work with files and folders, including

- **Finding your way around files and folders:** This includes tasks such as locating and opening files and folders.

- **Manipulating files and folders:** These tasks cover moving, renaming, and deleting a file.

- **Compressing a file:** This squeezes a file's contents to make larger files more manageable.

Get ready to . . .

Find and Open Files and Folders with Windows Explorer

1. To find and open a file, you use Windows Explorer, a feature of Windows that helps you locate files and folders stored on your computer or discs. (Windows Explorer is introduced in Chapter 3.) To open Windows Explorer, move your mouse pointer over the Start button and right-click. In the menu that appears, click Explore.

2. In the resulting Windows Explorer window, click the arrow to the left of any folder to display its contents in the left panel. This changes the arrow to point downward and reveals an outline of the hierarchy of folders, subfolders, and files. You can click the arrow again to hide the folder contents.

3. Click a subfolder in the left pane, as shown in Figure 10-1, and the subfolder opens to reveal its contents in the main display to the right.

4. If necessary, follow the procedure in Step 3 to open a series of folders until you locate the file you want.

5. When you find the file you want, double-click it, and it opens within the program used to create it.

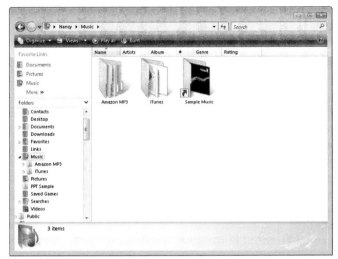

Figure 10-1: Folders, subfolders, and files

The Start menu includes some shortcuts to commonly used folders, including Documents, Pictures, and Music. Click one of these, and Windows Explorer opens with the contents of that particular folder displayed and ready for you to get to work.

Choose a File or Folder View

1. You can use the Views menu to see different perspectives and information about files in Windows Explorer. For example, you can see a simple list or view files and folders as graphical icons. First open Windows Explorer. (See the preceding task for an explanation of how to do this.)

2. Click the arrow on the Views button to display the menu, as shown in Figure 10-2, and choose one of the following menu options:

   - **Extra Large, Large, Medium, or Small Icons** displays a graphical symbol for each item.

   - **List** displays a list of folder and file names with no further information.

   - **Details** shows a list of folders and files that shows information such as Date Modified and Size (see Figure 10-3).

   - **Tiles** shows the file/folder name, dimensions, and size.

 If you're working with a folder containing graphics files, the graphics automatically display as thumbnails unless you choose Details. *Thumbnails* are small renditions of the actual graphic image contained in the file.

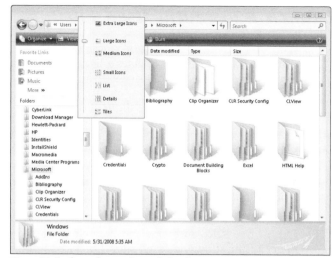

Figure 10-2: Choose the view that works best for you

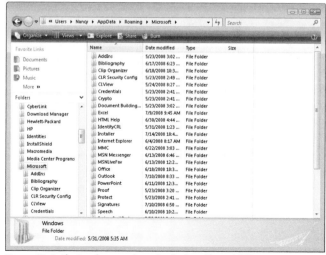

Figure 10-3: The Details view with, er, details about files and folders

Launch a Recently Used File

1. Windows provides a shortcut to opening files you worked with recently. It provides a listing of the most recently used files that you access through the Start menu. Right-click the Start button and choose Properties from the resulting shortcut menu.

2. In the Taskbar and Start Menu Properties dialog box that appears, click the Start Menu tab (if that tab isn't already displayed).

3. Make sure that the Store and Display a List of Recently Opened Files check box is selected (see Figure 10-4) and then click OK.

4. Choose Start⇨Recent Items and then choose a file from the resulting submenu (see Figure 10-5) to open it.

 If a file in the Recent Items list can be opened with more than one application — for example, a graphics file that you might open with Paint or in the Windows Picture and Fax Viewer — you can right-click the file and use the Open With command to control which application is used to open the file.

 If you open a new or recently used file and make changes, you should save the file.

Figure 10-4: Activating the recently opened files feature

Figure 10-5: The submenu of recently used files

Create a New Folder

1. Creating your own folders helps you organize your files exactly as you want them. To begin creating a new folder from within Windows Explorer, first right-click the Start button and choose Explore.

2. In the Windows Explorer window that appears, notice the Folders list on the left. Click the folder in which you want to create a new folder. For example, the Music folder.

3. On the Explorer toolbar, click Organize (near the top-left of the window) and click New Folder in the menu. A new folder appears in the list of file/folder names, with the default name of New Folder. The folder name is highlighted, indicating that the name is open for you to edit with your specific folder name (see Figure 10-6).

4. Type a folder name; the words New Folder are replaced with the name you type. Click anywhere outside the folder name to save it.

 If you happen to click outside the folder name before you start Step 4 or if you want to rename a folder at some later time, simply perform the steps in the following task, "Rename a File or Folder."

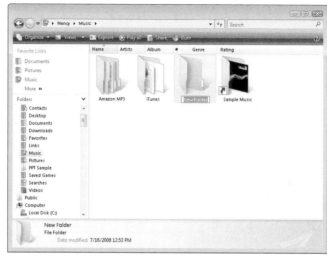

Figure 10-6: Name your new folder with a relevant title

Rename a File or Folder

1. As you work with your computer and add more and more files, you may find that you want to rename a file. For example you may have named a file "Taxes" but the next year you realize that you would be better off with a "2008 Taxes" and "2009 Taxes" folder. To rename a file or folder, open Windows Explorer by right-clicking Start and choosing Explore.

2. In Windows Explorer, locate the file or folder that you want to rename. (The task "Find and Open Files and Folders with Windows Explorer," earlier in this chapter, explains how.)

3. Right-click a file or folder in any pane and choose Rename (see Figure 10-7).

4. The file/folder name is now highlighted, indicating that it is available for editing. Type a new name and then click anywhere outside the file/folder name to save the new name.

 You can't rename a file to have the same name as another file of the same format located in the same folder. For example, you can't have two .doc files (which are word processed documents) of the same name in the same folder. Subfolders can't have the same name either.

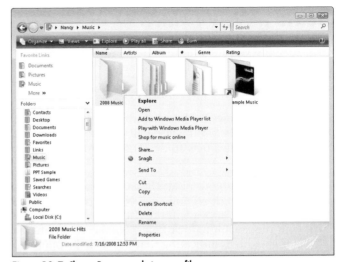

Figure 10-7: Choose Rename and give your file a new name

Search for a File

1. Even if you've proven to be a whiz at organizing files within folders, there will be times when you can't locate a file because you forgot the name or where you saved it. To find a file, choose Start.

2. In the Start Search field in the bottom-left corner of the Start menu, enter a search term. By default, all criteria for files are searched. In this example, I searched music, so any file with music in fields such as the filename, folder name, artist, album, or file type would be returned. The search begins, and the Start menu displays the results (see Figure 10-8). Windows searches only your computer by default — Windows won't search the Internet unless you click the Search the Internet link at the bottom of the results window.

3. To open a file at this point, you can simply click it.

4. If you want to search the Internet, click the Search the Internet link. Search results from Google appear in your default browser window (see Figure 10-9).

5. Click any search result item to go to that Web site.

 If you don't need the more advanced search features, you can also simply click Start and type your search term into the Start Search field at the bottom of the Start menu.

Figure 10-8: The Start menu with search results displayed

Figure 10-9: The results of searching the Internet from the Start menu

Add a File or Folder to Your Favorites List

1. The Windows Start menu offers a list of Favorites; these are Web sites, files, or folders that you like to work with often. Web sites are placed here when you add them as Favorites in Internet Explorer, which you read about in Chapter 16. To add files and folders to Favorites so you can access them quickly, first open Windows Explorer by right-clicking Start and choosing Explore.

2. In the resulting Windows Explorer window, locate the Web site, file, or folder that you want to make a Favorite. (The task "Find and Open Files and Folders with Windows Explorer," earlier in this chapter, explains how.)

3. Click the file or folder and hold down the mouse button as you drag it to the Favorites folder in the Folders list on the left (see Figure 10-10). You may have to scroll down the Folders list to find the Favorites folder. A copy of the item is placed in the Favorites folder.

4. To see a list of your Favorites, choose Start⇨Favorites.

5. In the resulting submenu (see Figure 10-11), click an item to open it.

 If the Favorites item doesn't display on your Start menu, right-click the Start menu and choose Properties. On the Start Menu tab, select the Start Menu radio button, and then click the Customize button. In the list in the Customize Start Menu dialog box that appears, make sure that Favorites Menu check box is selected, and then click OK twice to save the setting.

Figure 10-10: Adding a file to the Favorites folder

Figure 10-11: The Favorites submenu

Copy a File or Folder

1. You might want to create a copy of a file to save a backup of it in case the first file is damaged, to use it in another project, or to provide the copy to somebody else. To locate a file or folder to copy, right-click the Start button and choose Explore.

2. In the resulting Windows Explorer window, in the Folders list on the left, click the folder where the file you want to copy is located. If the file or folder you want is in a subfolder, click that folder to access it.

3. When you locate the file or folder you want to copy, right-click it and choose Copy from the shortcut menu that appears (see Figure 10-12).

4. Navigate to the folder where you want to copy the file or folder (for example, a different folder in the Folder list).

5. Right-click in the Windows Explorer pane that lists files and folders and choose Paste (see Figure 10-13). A copy of the file is pasted into that location.

 You can also select a file and then, using the Explorer toolbar, choose Organize⇨Copy to perform the copy function and Organize⇨Paste to perform the paste function.

Figure 10-12: Choose Copy from the shortcut menu

Figure 10-13: Paste your copied item into another folder

Move a File or Folder

1. If you decide a file or folder should be stored in another location, you can simply move it. To get started, right-click the Start button and choose Explore.

2. In the resulting Windows Explorer window (see Figure 10-14), click a folder or series of folders to locate the file that you want to move.

3. Click the file and hold down the mouse button as you drag the file to another folder in the Folders list on the left side of the window. If you right-click and drag the item to a new location, when you release the mouse button, you're offered the options of moving or copying the item when you place it via a shortcut menu that appears.

4. Click the Close button in the upper-right corner of the Windows Explorer window to close it.

 If you change your mind about moving an item using the right-click-and-drag method, you can click Cancel on the shortcut menu that appears.

Figure 10-14: Locate the file or folder that you want to move

Create a Compressed File or Folder

1. To make a large file more manageable, you can compress it (much like using a trash compactor to minimize your trash). Open Windows Explorer by right-clicking Start and choosing Explore.

2. In the resulting Windows Explorer window, locate the files or folders that you want to compress. (The task "Find and Open Files and Folders with Windows Explorer," earlier in this chapter, explains how.)

3. Now you need to select what you want to compress. For this step, you can do either of the following:

   • **Select a series of files or folders:** Click a file or folder, press and hold the Shift key, and then click another file or folder to select a series of items listed consecutively. The first and last items and all items in between are selected.

   • **Select nonconsecutive items (as shown in Figure 10-15):** Press and hold the Ctrl key and click each item you want to include. All the individual items you clicked are selected.

4. Right-click any one of the selected items. In the resulting shortcut menu (see Figure 10-16), choose Send To⇨ Compressed (Zipped) Folder. A new compressed folder appears. The folder icon is named after the last file you selected in the series, and the name of the folder is left open for you to edit.

5. To rename your brand-new compressed file, just type a new name and then click outside of the filename area. (To rename the file at a later time, see the task "Rename a File or Folder," earlier in this chapter.)

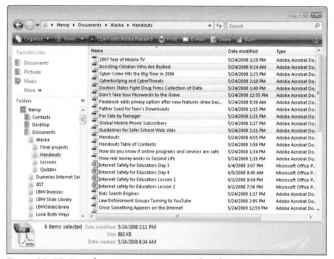

Figure 10-15: Several nonconsecutive items are selected

Figure 10-16: Sending the selected items to a compressed folder

Delete a File or Folder

1. Just as you sometimes clean out your closet of clothes you no longer wear, there's just no good reason to keep old, unused files or folders around. To delete files or folders, start by right-clicking the Start button and choosing Explore.

2. In the resulting Windows Explorer window, locate the file or folder you want to delete. (The task "Find and Open Files and Folders with Windows Explorer" explains how.)

3. Right-click the file or folder to open a shortcut menu (see Figure 10-17) and then choose Delete.

4. The resulting dialog box asks whether you're sure you want to delete the file. Click Yes to confirm the deletion.

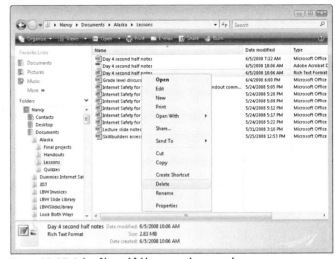

Figure 10-17: Delete files and folders you no longer need

 When you delete a file or folder in Windows Vista, it's not really gone. It's moved to the Recycle Bin folder. Windows Vista periodically purges older files from this folder when it gets too full, but you might still be able to retrieve recently deleted files and folders from it. To try to restore a deleted file or folder, double-click the Recycle Bin icon on the desktop. Right-click the file or folder and choose Restore. Windows Vista restores the file to wherever it was when you deleted it.

Back Up Files to a Writable CD or DVD

1. To begin actually creating your backup, place a blank writable CD-R/RW (read/writable) or DVD-R/RW in your CD-ROM or DVD-ROM drive. You usually open the drive by pressing a button on the front of the drive and close it again by pushing the drive back in. Alternatively, you can insert a USB flash drive to back up to (see Chapter 3 for more details).

2. Choose Start➪Documents.

3. In the resulting Documents window, select all the files that you want to copy to disc by clicking one and then, while holding down the Ctrl key, clicking all other files one by one (see Figure 10-18).

4. Click the Burn button.

5. In the Burn a Disc dialog box that appears, enter a disc title and click Next.

6. A pop-up appears near the taskbar (see Figure 10-19), indicating that you have files waiting to be burned. Click it and a window appears. Click the Burn to Disc button. When the files have been copied, click the Close button to close the CD-R/RW-ROM or DVD-ROM window.

 If you want to back up the entire contents of a folder, such as the Document folder, you can just click the Documents folder itself in Step 2.

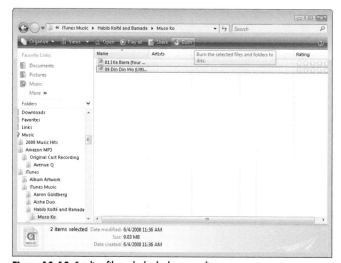

Figure 10-18: Sending files to be backed up on a disc

Figure 10-19: Burning files to a disc

Working with Software

The whole point of that computer sitting on your desk (or floor, or lap) is to run software programs. Software ranges from the coolest new game with wow graphics to get-down-to-business spreadsheet or word-processing programs. However, all software programs have some things in common.

First, unless a program comes already loaded on your computer, you have to install it. Conversely, if there is software on your computer you don't need (you know, like that tax program you used in 2000 that's been hanging around for years), you can remove it. Then you should master features in Windows for starting, closing, and switching between running programs.

Windows Vista is software, too (software that runs your other software, among other things). You can take advantage of several pieces of software that you get with Windows to work with words, pictures, contacts, or little tools called gadgets that are part of Windows Sidebar.

Install Software

1. Insert a software CD/DVD into your computer's CD drive or DVD drive.

2. Follow the instructions that appear on-screen (see Figure 11-1) to begin the installation. Typically you would click on an option to Run the setup.exe file, which is the software installation file, though some software will display a proprietary dialog box for running its software installation.

3. If a prompt appears asking for permission to run the program, click Allow.

4. An installation wizard may appear (see Figure 11-2) asking you to respond to certain questions about the installation, or a progress dialog box may appear showing that the installation has begun without any input from you. In some cases you will be asked to agree to terms and conditions before being allowed to proceed with the installation.

5. When you're notified that the installation is complete, click the appropriate button (usually labeled something like Finish, OK, or Done).

 If the installation doesn't proceed along the lines described here, you may have to do a manual install. Check the documentation for the software to see how to do this. It usually involves finding a file named Setup.exe on the CD/DVD provided by the software manufacturer and double-clicking it to being the installation.

Figure 11-1: Choose to run the setup file

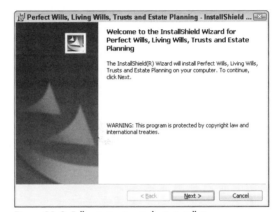

Figure 11-2: Follow instructions to begin installation

Uninstall Software

1. Your computer comes to you with certain programs pre-installed, either by the manufacturer or a previous user. You won't necessarily want to keep every program and you'll want to install others that are useful to you, so it's handy to know how to uninstall unwanted software applications. Choose Start➪Control Panel➪Uninstall a Program (under the Programs category).

2. In the resulting Uninstall or Change a Program window, as shown in Figure 11-3, select the program that you want to get rid of.

3. Click the Uninstall or Uninstall/Change button. (The button you have to click will vary somewhat depending on the program you select.) Although some programs display their own uninstall screens that give you instructions to follow for how to remove the program, in most cases, a confirmation dialog box appears (see Figure 11-4).

4. If you're sure that you want to remove the program, click Yes in the confirmation dialog box. A dialog box shows the progress of the procedure; it disappears when the program has been uninstalled.

5. Click the Close button to close the Uninstall or Change a Program window.

 With some programs that include multiple applications, such as Microsoft Office, you might want to remove only one program, not the whole shooting match. For example, you might decide that you have no earthly use for Access but can't let a day go by without using Excel and Word — so why not free up some hard drive space and send Access packing? If you have a program that you can modify in this way, you see a Change button in Step 2 of this task in addition to the Uninstall button. Click Change. A dialog box appears to allow you to select the programs that you want to install or uninstall; in some cases, Windows might open the original installation screen from your software program.

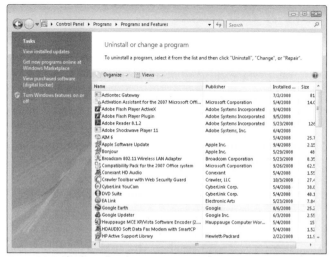

Figure 11-3: The Uninstall or Change a Program window

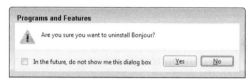

Figure 11-4: Confirm the uninstall

 Warning: If you click the Uninstall button, some programs are simply removed with no further input from you. Be really sure that you don't need a program before you remove it or that you have the original software on a CD or DVD so you can reinstall it should you need it again.

Start a Program

1. Before you can use a program you have to start it (also called *launching* a program). Launch a program by using any of the following four methods:

   - Press the Windows key on your keyboard and choose All Programs. Locate the program name in the All Programs list that appears and click it. Clicking an item with a folder icon displays a list of programs within it; just click the program on that sublist to open it (as shown in Figure 11-5).

   - Double-click a program shortcut icon on the desktop (see Figure 11-6).

   - Click a program icon on the Quick Launch bar, located on the taskbar. The taskbar should display by default; if it doesn't, press the Windows key (on your keyboard) to display it, and then click an icon on the Quick Launch bar, just to the right of the Start button. If the Quick Launch bar is not displayed, see the task on customizing the Quick Launch bar in Chapter 8 for details.

   - If you used the program recently and saved a document, choose Recent Items from the Start menu. Then click a document created in that program from the list that displays. (See Chapter 10 for information about displaying recently used files on the Start menu.)

2. When the application opens, if it's a game, play it; if it's a spreadsheet, enter numbers into it; if it's your e-mail program, start deleting junk mail . . . you get the idea.

Figure 11-5: Choose a program from the Start menu

Figure 11-6: Desktop shortcuts

Switch between Open Programs

1. You can have two or more programs, or two or more windows in a single program, open on your desktop. The last program that you worked in is the active program. To switch between open programs easily, hold down the Alt key and then press Tab.

2. A small box opens, as shown in Figure 11-7, revealing all opened programs.

3. Release the Tab key but keep Alt pressed down. Press Tab to cycle through the icons representing open programs.

4. When you release the Alt key, Windows Vista switches to whichever program is selected. To switch back to the last program that was active, simply press Alt+Tab, and that program becomes the active program once again.

Microsoft Excel - Book1

Figure 11-7: Press Tab to move among open programs

 All open programs also appear as items on the Windows Vista taskbar. Just click any running program on the taskbar to display that window and make it the active program. If the taskbar isn't visible, press the Windows key on your keyboard to display the taskbar.

Close a Program

1. When you're done with a program, you might as well close it. With an application open, first save any open documents and then close the application by using one of these methods:

    *   **Click the Close button** in the upper-right corner of the window. If two or more instances of the program are open in separate windows, this closes the document and its current window but not the application.

    *   **Choose File⊃Exit** (see Figure 11-8). Note that if you're using a Microsoft Office 2007 program you click the Office button and then click the Exit [Name of Application] button.

2. The application closes. If you haven't saved any documents before trying to close the application, you see a dialog box asking whether you want to save the document. Click Yes or No, depending on whether you want to save your changes.

 Note that choosing File⊃Exit closes all open documents in an application as well as the application. Choose File⊃Close to close only the currently active document and keep the application and any other open documents open.

Figure 11-8: Using the File menu to exit a program

 To save a document before closing an application, choose File⊃Save and use settings in the Save As dialog box that appears to name the file and also specify which folder to save it to.

Set Up Windows Sidebar

1. To get started with the Sidebar and the useful gadgets that it holds, click the Sidebar icon on the Windows taskbar to instantly display the Sidebar at any time.

2. If the icon doesn't appear on the taskbar, choose Start➪Control Panel➪Appearance and Personalization➪Choose whether to Keep Sidebar on Top of Other Windows (in the Windows Sidebar Properties category) to open the Windows Sidebar Properties dialog box (see Figure 11-9).

3. Select the Sidebar Is Always on Top of Other Windows check box. If you like, you can also enable the Start Sidebar When Windows Starts option to ensure that the Sidebar always displays when you start your computer.

4. Click OK and the Control Panel window closes. The Sidebar appears, as shown in Figure 11-10.

5. Click a displayed gadget and drag it to the desktop if you want it to stay there even when the Sidebar is closed.

 If you're left-handed or have some other propensity for things on the left, you can choose to have the Sidebar displayed on the left side of the screen by selecting the Left radio button in the Windows Sidebar Properties dialog box.

Figure 11-9: The Windows Sidebar Properties dialog box

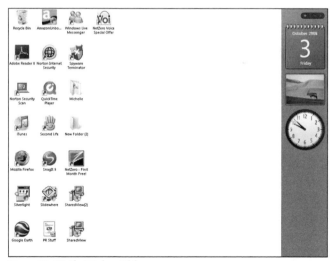

Figure 11-10: The Windows Sidebar

Add Gadgets to the Sidebar

1. To display more gadgets, click the Gadgets symbol (a plus sign) at the top of the Sidebar.

2. In the resulting Add Gadgets dialog box (see Figure 11-11), double-click a gadget (or click and drag it to the Sidebar). If you need to view additional gadgets, click the Get More Gadgets Online link in the lower-right corner of the dialog box.

3. Click the Close button to close the dialog box.

 If you display gadgets and then click and drag them onto the desktop, even if you close the Sidebar, they stay visible. So if you want to save desktop space, find the gadgets you like, plop them on your desktop, and hide the Sidebar! To close the Sidebar, right-click anywhere in it and choose Close Sidebar.

 If you add more gadgets than can be shown in the single Sidebar, use the Previous and Next arrows at the top of the Sidebar to move from one set of gadgets to the next.

Figure 11-11: The Add Gadgets dialog box

Create and Format a Document in WordPad

1. Choose Start⇨All Programs⇨Accessories⇨WordPad.

2. Enter text in the blank document, as shown in Figure 11-12. (Note: Press Enter to create blank lines between paragraphs.)

3. Click and drag over text to select it and then choose Format⇨Font.

4. In the resulting Font dialog box (see Figure 11-13), adjust the settings for Font, Font Style, or Size; apply strikeout (strikethrough) or underline effects by selecting those check boxes. You can also modify the font color. Click OK to apply the settings.

5. Select text and click various other tools (such as the alignment buttons or the bullet style button) on the toolbar to format selected text.

6. When your document is complete, choose File⇨Save. In the Save As dialog box, enter a name in the File Name text box, select a file location from the Save In drop-down list, and then click Save.

 E-mailing a copy of your WordPad document to a friend is simple. Just choose File⇨Send, and an e-mail form appears from your default e-mail program with the file already attached. Just enter a recipient's address and message and then click Send. It's on its way!

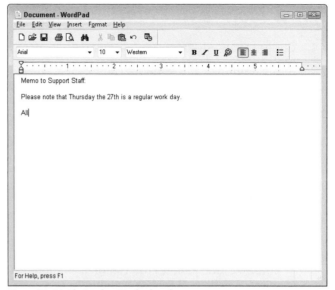

Figure 11-12: The Windows WordPad window

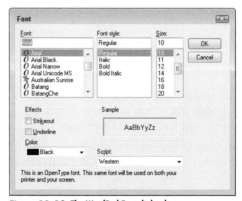

Figure 11-13: The WordPad Font dialog box

Edit a Picture in Paint

1. Choose Start⇨All Programs⇨Accessories⇨Paint.

2. In the resulting Paint window, choose File⇨Open. Locate a picture file that you want to edit (as in Figure 11-14), select it, and then click Open. A pretty picture of my cats is shown in the Paint window in Figure 11-15.

3. Now you can edit the picture in any number of ways:

   - **Edit colors.** Choose a color from the color palette in the bottom-left corner and use various tools (such as an Airbrush, Brush, Fill With Color, or the Color Dropper tools) to apply color to the image or selected objects such as rectangles.

   - **Select areas.** Select the Free-Form Select and Select tools and then click and drag on the image to select a portion of the picture. You can then crop out your selected element by choosing Edit⇨Cut.

   - **Add Text.** Select the Text Tool and then click and drag on the image to create a text box in which you can enter and format text.

   - **Draw objects.** Select the Rectangle, Rounded Rectangle, Polygon, or Ellipse tool, and then click and drag the image to draw objects.

   - **Modify the image.** Use the commands on the Image menu to change the colors and stretch out, flip around, or change the size of the image.

4. Choose File⇨Save to save your masterpiece; choose File⇨Print to print it, or choose File⇨Send to send it by e-mail.

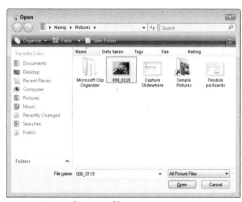

Figure 11-14: Choosing a file to open

Figure 11-15: A picture open in Paint

Enter Information in the Windows Contacts

1. Choose Start⇨All Programs⇨Windows Contacts. You might get a dialog box asking whether you want to make this your default vCard (an electronic business card) viewer. Click Yes or No depending on your preference.

2. In the Contact Properties dialog box that appears (see Figure 11-16) enter information in various fields, clicking other tabs to add more details. For some fields, such as E-Mail Address, you must enter information and then click the Add button to add it to your contact properties.

3. When you finish entering information, click OK.

 If the contact has more than one e-mail address, select the one you want to most often send e-mail to and then click the Set as Default button. This is the address any e-mails to that contact will be addressed to.

 To quickly search your Contacts, choose Start and enter the contact name in the Search Field. The contact name appears in the Start menu. Click it to open the contact Properties form.

Figure 11-16: The Contact Properties dialog box

Working with Networks

Chapter 12

Setting up a network among two or more computers can make your life much easier because after you set up that network, you can use the connection to share files, folders, printers, and access to the Internet among the connected computers.

One common way to connect a network is to use a wired Ethernet connection, involving cables and equipment, referred to as a *hub* or *switch*. Check the back of your PC. You should see what looks like a very large phone connector jack. This is the *Ethernet connector.*

After you connect the necessary cables and equipment, most newer computers already have network drivers installed, so Windows Vista is capable of recognizing the connection. With simple-to-use wizards, little input on your part is required to set up a network.

You can also set up a connection through a wireless access point (which you set up according to the instructions that come with the wireless router) with an adapter that you either install in your CPU in the form of a PCI adapter or plug into your PC by using a USB (Universal Serial Bus) port.

In this chapter, you explore the following tasks:

- Setting up a wired Ethernet connection
- Setting up a wireless access point and configuring a wireless network using the Wireless Network Setup Wizard
- Making various settings to networked computers such as changing a computer's network name and joining a network workgroup

Get ready to . . .

Set Up a Wired Ethernet Network

1. Obtain a Cat 5 or Cat 5e Ethernet cable for every computer you want to connect to the network (see Figure 12-1).

2. Purchase a hub or switch with enough ports for each computer you want to connect (see Figure 12-2).

3. Turn off all computers as well as the switch or hub. Plug one end of the Ethernet cable into the switch or hub and the other end into the network adapter in your PC.

4. Repeat Step 3 for each computer you want to include in the network.

5. Turn on the switch or hub and then turn on the computers. You can now use the Network Setup Wizard to set up the network. (Choose Start⇨Network, and then click the Network and Sharing Center button. In the resulting Network and Sharing Center window, click the Set Up a Connection or Network link.)

 Switches make for a speedier network, although they cost a little more than a hub. However, in most cases, it's better to invest a few dollars more for the extra performance of a switch. If you want to get very sophisticated — for example, on a company network — you could use a router, which helps you track various people on the network.

 Cat 5 is a kind of cable used for data transfer. If your home is wired for high-speed access, you may have Cat 5 cable in your walls. You can find the kind of Cat 5 cable referred to in this task at your local computer or office supply store with connectors for plugging into your computer and hub.

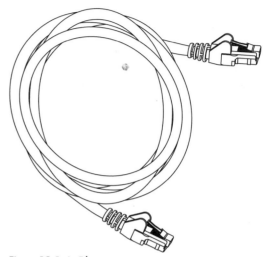

Figure 12-1: An Ethernet connector

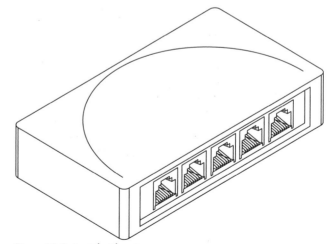

Figure 12-2: A switch with ports

Connect to a Network

1. Once you've set up your network, to connect a computer with appropriate permissions, click the Windows key and then right-click the Networks icon in the System tray of the taskbar and choose Connect to a Network.

2. In the resulting Connect to a Network window (see Figure 12-3), click the network name and then click Connect.

3. At this point, you have two options:

   • **If the network is unsecured,** you see a message like the one shown in Figure 12-4 that warns you that the network is unsecured and you can click Connect Anyway to proceed.

   • **If the network is security-enabled,** you see a window asking you to enter the security key or passphrase. Enter the key or passphrase and click Connect. A window appears to tell you that you have successfully connected to the network.

 Occasionally you'll see a message that you can't connect to a network at this time. This can be caused by a few different conditions. First, the network signal may be too weak for some reason, Second, the network server might be experiencing some problems. In some cases, moving your computer closer to the network router in your home might help, or you can simply wait a while and try the connection again. There are also wireless boosters you can buy that you can place between the wireless router and a PC to boost the signal.

Figure 12-3: The Connect to a Network window

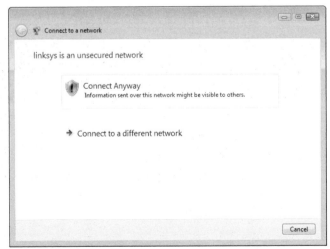

Figure 12-4: A warning that a network is unsecured

Change a Computer's Network Name

1. If you like, you can change your computer's name on a network. Choose Start⇨Control Panel⇨System and Maintenance and then click the System link.

2. In the resulting System window, as shown in Figure 12-5, click the Change Settings link.

3. On the Computer Name tab of the resulting System Properties dialog box, as shown in Figure 12-6, replace the current name in the Computer Description text box with another network name and then click OK to save the new name.

4. Click the Close button to close the System Properties dialog box.

 Two computers on the same network cannot have the same name. Therefore, you may want to modify computer names before you start setting up your network so that they're unique. Choose Start⇨Control Panel⇨System and Maintenance and click the System link. In the System dialog box click Advanced System Settings, and then display the Computer Name tab. Enter the name in the Computer Description field. Making the computer name descriptive is useful. Simple names such as John's Computer and Basement PC help everybody on the network know which is which.

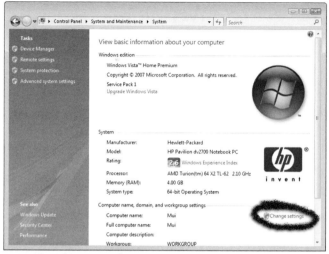

Figure 12-5: The System window

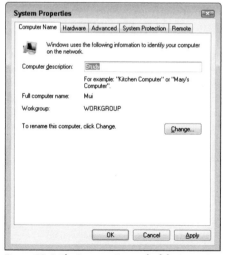

Figure 12-6: The Computer Name tab of the System Properties dialog box

Join a Workgroup

1. For computers on a network to recognize each other, they need to belong to the same workgroup. To change a workgroup association, choose Start⇨Control Panel⇨ System and Maintenance and then click the System Link.

2. In the resulting System dialog box, click the Change Settings link.

3. On the Computer Name tab of the resulting System Properties dialog box, shown in Figure 12-7, click the Change button.

4. The Computer Name Changes dialog box appears (see Figure 12-8). In the Workgroup field, enter or edit the name for your workgroup with no spaces between letters.

5. Click OK to close the dialog box and then click OK again to close the System Properties dialog box. If prompted, restart Windows Vista.

 A workgroup is essentially a set of computers on a network. On a large network, breaking computers down into these groups so they can easily work with each other makes sense. In a smaller, home network, you will probably just create one workgroup to allow all your computers to easily access each other.

 One task that becomes easier when your computer is part of a workgroup is sharing files. If you locate a file or folder on your computer and right-click it, you can choose to share it on the network. When you do, only people using computers that are in your workgroup will be able to access this shared file or folder.

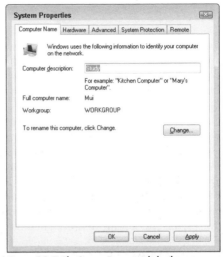

Figure 12-7: The System Properties dialog box

Figure 12-8: The Computer Name Changes dialog box

Work with Wireless Networks

1. Turn on each PC that you have attached to the network.

2. On the PC that will share its Internet connection, log on to the Internet.

3. On the Internet-connected PC, choose Start⇨Network and then click the Network and Sharing Center button.

4. In the resulting Network and Sharing Center window, click the Set Up a Connection or Network link.

5. In the resulting Choose a Connection Option window (see Figure 12-9), choose the Set Up a Wireless Router or Access Point option and then click Next. The next window describes what the wizard will do; click Next.

 If you don't have all the PCs to be networked available, you can add a computer to the network at a later time by running this procedure again. Or, you can use the settings you save to a flash drive (see following steps) to set up a single computer at a later time.

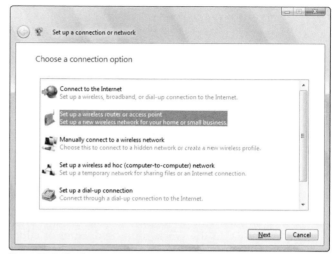

Figure12-9: The Choose a Connection Option window

6. A progress window displays (see Figure 12-10) while Windows Vista detects your hardware settings. You have a few options at this point:

- Windows Vista detects your hardware and configures it automatically; you're done.

- Windows Vista detects your hardware but requires you to configure it manually. In this case, select the Configure This Device Manually option and complete the required information to finish the setup.

- If you have a Flash drive connected via a USB port, connect the drive and click the Create Wireless Network Settings and Save to a USB Flash Drive option. Enter a name for your network on the following screen and then follow the directions, which involve disconnecting the Flash drive and plugging it into a wireless access point. You can then use the drive to configure each computer on the network as directed.

7. On the final wizard screen that appears, click Finish.

 One great feature of using a network is that you can share things. You can share files and folders, and you can even share your CD/DVD drive for little laptops that don't have those drives installed.

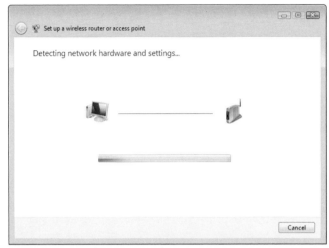

Figure 12-10: A Windows progress window

Having Fun with Photos and Movies

*T*he ability to manipulate images and work with movies provides a wonderful way to entertain and communicate. Your computer makes it possible for you to watch movies, create your own movies, and view and manipulate photos using built-in Windows applications.

You discover a variety of multimedia-related tasks in this chapter, including

➡ Playing movies with Windows Media Player

➡ Working with movies in Windows Movie Maker

➡ Uploading photos from your digital camera

➡ Using Windows Photo Gallery for viewing and editing photos

➡ Burning photos to a CD or DVD

Chapter
13

Get ready to . . .

Play Movies with Windows Media Player

1. To open Windows Media Player and begin working with movie files, choose Start⇨All Programs⇨ Windows Media Player.

2. Click the Maximize button in the resulting Media Player window. (Maximize is in the upper-right corner of the window, next to the X-shaped Close button, sporting two square icons.)

3. Click the arrow on the bottom of the Library button at the top of the window and click Video.

4. In the window listing video files that appear, click the Library folder that contains the movie you want to play (as shown in Figure 13-1).

5. Double-click a file to begin the playback (see Figure 13-2). Use tools at the bottom of the screen to do the following:

   - Adjust the volume of any sound track by clicking and dragging the slider left (to make it softer) or right (to make it louder). Click the megaphone-shaped volume icon to mute the sound (and click it again to turn the sound back on).

   - Pause the playback by clicking the round Pause button in the center of the toolbar.

   - Stop the playback by clicking the square-shaped Stop button toward the left.

   - Skip to the next or previous movie by clicking the arrow buttons to the left or right of the Pause button.

6. Click the Close button to close Media Player.

Figure 13-1: The Library folder containing videos for playback

Figure 13-2: The video playback window

Create a New Project in Windows Movie Maker

1. Choose Start⇨All Programs⇨ Windows Movie Maker to open the Movie Maker window.

2. Choose File⇨New Project to open a new blank Movie Maker file.

3. Click the Import Media button to open the Import Media Items dialog box.

4. Use the Look In drop-down list to locate the folder where the movie file you want to open is saved.

5. Click the file and then click Import to open the file in the Movie Maker window, as shown in Figure 13-3. (*Note:* You can repeat this procedure to open more than one movie file in a project.)

6. Click clips displayed in the Collection pane and drag them down to the storyboard along the bottom of the window, as shown in Figure 13-4.

7. Choose File⇨Save Project. In the Save Project As dialog box, enter a filename in the File Name text box and then click Save.

 After you create a project, what can you actually do with it? When you've created a project and imported movies into it, you can use various features of Movie Maker to edit, reorganize, and playback movies. With more than one movie imported into a project, for example, you could pick and choose clips from each of them and organize them to create your own unique movie.

 Another nice feature when playing back movies in Windows Movie Maker is the ability to view movies with the full screen by clicking the Full Screen button. Press Esc to exit the Full Screen mode.

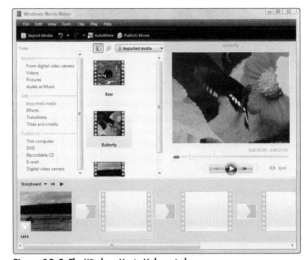

Figure 13-3: The Windows Movie Maker window

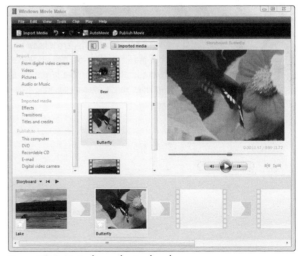

Figure 13-4: Movie clips on the storyboard

Add Video Effects to a Movie

1. With a movie open in Movie Maker, choose Tools➪Effects.

2. In the Effects pane, as shown in Figure 13-5, click an effect and drag it to a clip in your movie on the storyboard or timeline. A star appears on a clip to indicate that it has an effect applied.

3. To add several affects to a selected clip at once, choose Clip➪Video➪Effects.

4. In the Add or Remove Effects dialog box, as shown in Figure 13-6, click any effect in the list on the left and then click Add. To remove an effect, click any effect in the list on the right and then click Remove.

5. When you're finished, click OK. When you click the Play button to play the video, you can view your stunning effects.

 Note that some of the effects are available only if you purchase Microsoft Plus! If you select one of those effects, a window pops up informing you of this and providing a link to a Web site where you can purchase this software to download or ship to you for about $20. Microsoft Plus! includes various media-enhancing tools and clips.

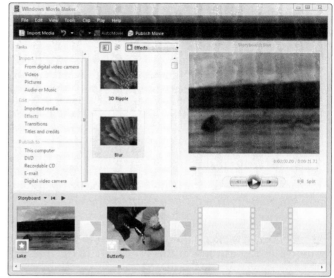

Figure 13-5: The Effects pane

Figure 13-6: The Add or Remove Effects dialog box

Upload Photos from Your Digital Camera

Uploading photos from a camera to your computer is a very simple process, but it helps to understand what's involved. (This is similar to the process you can use to upload movies from a camcorder — in both cases, check your manual for details.) Here are some highlights:

➡ **Making the connection:** Uploading photos from a digital camera to a computer requires that you connect the camera to a USB port on your computer using a USB cable, which typically comes with the camera. When you make this connection you'll see a dialog box like the one shown in Figure 13-7.

➡ **Installing software:** Digital cameras also typically come with software that makes uploading photos to your computer easy. Install the software and then follow the easy-to-use interface to upload photos. If you're missing such software, you can simply connect your camera to your computer and use Windows Explorer to locate the camera device on your computer and copy and paste photo files into a folder on your hard drive. (Chapter 3 tells you how to use Windows Explorer.)

➡ **Printing straight from the camera:** Some cameras save photos onto a memory card, and many printers include a slot where you can insert the memory card from the camera and print directly from it without having to first upload pictures (see Figure 13-8). Some cameras also connect directly to printers. However, if you want to keep a copy of the photo and clear up space in your camera's memory, you should upload it to your computer, even if you can print without uploading.

Figure 13-7: Importing pictures from a camera

Figure 13-8: A printer with slots for printing photos

View a Digital Image in Windows Photo Gallery

1. After you upload your photos to your computer, you can view them on-screen. To begin, choose Start⇨ All Programs⇨Windows Photo Gallery.

2. In the resulting Windows Photo Gallery window, as shown in Figure 13-9, click any of the items in the Navigation pane on the left to choose which images to display (such as those saved in a certain folder).

3. In the main area of the window, double-click an image to display it. Then use the tools at the bottom of the window (see Figure 13-10) to do any of the following:

   • The large rectangular icon in the middle is the **Play Slide Show** button. Click it to begin a slide show of your photos, played one after the other.

   • The **Display Size** icon, a little magnifying glass, displays a slider you can click and drag to change the size of the image thumbnails.

   • The **Actual Size/Fit In Window** icon, a small rectangle with four arrows around it's corners, allows you to toggle between the photo's actual dimensions and fitting the full photo within the viewing space.

   • The **Next** and **Previous** icons move to a previous or next image in the same folder.

   • The **Rotate Clockwise** and **Rotate Counterclockwise** icons spin the image 90 degrees at a time.

   • The **Delete** button deletes the selected image.

4. When you finish viewing images, click the Close button in the top-right corner to close the Photo Gallery.

Figure 13-9: Windows Photo Gallery

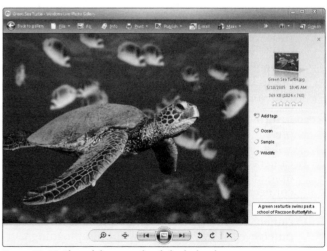

Figure 13-10: The tools let you work with the displayed image

Fix a Photo

Photo Gallery has tools for editing a photo, adjusting settings such as the photo brightness, and cropping to a portion of the image. If you use any of these tools and then change your mind about the edit, use the Undo tool at the bottom of the Fix pane. (If you change your mind *again*, use the Redo tool.) However, after you close the Fix pane, any changes you made and haven't undone are saved permanently.

Figure 13-11: The Fix window of Windows Photo Gallery

1. With the Photo Gallery open, display a photo by locating it with the Navigation pane. (See the task "View a Digital Image in Windows Photo Gallery," earlier in this chapter, for detailed steps if you need them.) Then click the thumbnail to select it.

2. Click the Fix button at the top of the Photo Gallery Window. The Fix window appears, as shown in Figure 13-11.

3. Click **Auto Adjust** to let Photo Gallery fix the photo or use any of the following tools. Click the tool name once to display options and click it again to close that tool.

   • Click **Adjust Exposure** and use the sliders to adjust brightness and contrast.

 The Undo feature in this window allows you to pick the action you want to undo, unlike many Undo features that force you to undo all the actions leading back to the action you want to undo. Click the arrow on the Undo button under the tools, rather than on the set of buttons along the bottom, to use this feature.

- Click **Adjust Color** and use the sliders (see Figure 13-12) to adjust temperature, tint, and saturation.

- Click **Crop Picture** and use the handles on the rectangle that appears to enlarge or shrink the area on the photo to be cropped. Alternatively, click the rectangle and drag it around your picture to crop to another location on it. Click the Apply button to apply the cropping.

- If your picture contains a face with red, glowing eyes, click the **Fix Red Eye** tool and then click and drag around the eye you want to fix in your image to adjust it.

4. You can use the navigation tools at the bottom to zoom in or out, fit the image to the window, move to the next image, undo or redo actions, or delete the picture. When you're finished, click the Back to Gallery button. All changes are saved permanently.

Figure 13-12: The Adjust Color tool of Windows Photo Gallery

 If you want to keep both the original version of your photo and the one to which you've applied effects, be sure to save the photo with a different name before using the Effects feature of Windows Photo Gallery.

Burn Photos to a CD or DVD

1. Insert a writable CD or DVD into your disc drive. (Discs come in read and write versions; you need a writable disc to save data to it and not just read data from it. See Chapter 3 for more about working with discs.)

2. With the Windows Media Player open, display a photo or music file by locating it with the Navigation pane.

3. Click the Burn button at the top of the application window, and then choose Audio CD or Data CD or DVD from the menu that appears, depending on whether you're burning music or video.

4. In the Disc pane that appears on the right (see Figure 13-13), drag items to burn to the CD or DVD into the pane.

5. Click Start Burn.

6. When the files have been burned to the disc, a confirmation dialog box appears, and your disc drawer opens. Click Finish to complete the process and close the wizard.

Figure 13-13: The Disc pane appears on the right

 In the confirmation dialog box that appears in Step 7, you can select the Yes, Burn These Files to Another Disc check box if you want to make another copy of the same files.

Working with Sound and Music

Who doesn't love to hear music? It soothes the savage beast and gets you dancing and singing. To spice up the sometimes-tedious time you spend working on your PC, add a dash of music! You can play music — or for that matter, any kind of audio file — from your computer and forget the iPod.

Your computer can play, record, and download music as well as tap into Internet radio stations with ease. With a sound card installed and speakers attached, you have a hi-tech desktop boombox. By using Windows Vista media programs, you can create playlists and even listen to your favorite radio station while working or playing on your desktop or laptop PC.

When you feel the need for sound, here's what your PC lets you do:

- ➡ Set up your sound card.
- ➡ Set up speakers.
- ➡ Set up your Windows Vista sound scheme.
- ➡ Download and play audio files.
- ➡ Create a playlist in Windows Media Player.
- ➡ Record music with Windows Sound Recorder.

Get ready to . . .

Set Up a Sound Card

1. Choose Start➪Control Panel➪Hardware and Sound, and then click the Manage Audio Devices link.

2. In the resulting Sound dialog box, which opens with the Playback tab sheet displayed, click the sound card that you want to modify and then click the Properties button (see Figure 14-1).

3. In the resulting Output Properties dialog box, as shown in Figure 14-2, click the arrow on the Device Usage drop-down list and choose the Use This Device (Enable) setting if it isn't already selected.

4. If you want to make sure you have the most current driver, click the Properties button and then, in the resulting dialog box on the Driver tab, click the Update Driver button.

5. When you're done making settings, click OK.

 Read your user's manual before doing this procedure. Some sound cards are built into the motherboard, but others require that you take some steps to disable the old card before installing the new.

 The Sound Troubleshooter, which you can access from the Windows Help and Support Troubleshooting system, takes you through testing your sound card step by step and isolating various problems. But remember the basics: You have to have speakers connected to your computer, and the volume setting on your computer can't be muted. If you neglect to properly set either of these two vital requirements, don't be ashamed — just about everyone has done it, myself included!

Figure 14-1: The Playback tab of the Sound dialog box

Figure 14-2: The General tab of the Output Properties dialog box

Set Up Speakers

1. Attach speakers to your computer by plugging them into the appropriate connection (often labeled with a little megaphone or speaker symbol) on your central processing unit (CPU) or monitor.

2. Choose Start⇨Control Panel⇨Hardware and Sound; in the Hardware and Sound window that appears, click the Manage Audio Devices link (under Sound).

3. In the resulting Sound dialog box, on the Playback tab (see Figure 14-3), double-click the Speakers item.

4. In the resulting Speakers Properties dialog box, click the Levels tab, as shown in Figure 14-4, and then click and drag the Speakers slider to adjust the speaker volume. Dragging the slider to the left lowers the volume; dragging to the right raises the volume. *Note:* If there's a small red *x* on the speaker button, click it to activate the speakers.

5. Click the Balance button. In the resulting Balance dialog box, use the L(eft) and R(ight) sliders to adjust the balance of sounds between the two speakers.

6. Click OK three times to close all the open dialog boxes and save the new settings.

You can easily test your speakers. On the Advanced tab of the Speakers Properties dialog box, choose your speaker configuration and then click the Test button. This feature tests first one speaker and then the other to help you pinpoint whether one of your speakers is having problems or whether you should adjust the balance between the speakers for better sound.

Figure 14-3: The Playback tab of the Sound dialog box

Figure 14-4: The Level tab of the Sound Properties dialog box

Configure Audio Volume

1. Choose Start➪Control Panel➪Hardware and Sound, and then click the Adjust System Volume link to display the Volume Mixer dialog box, as shown in Figure 14-5.

2. Under the Device volume section, adjust any of the following settings:

* **Volume sliders:** Move these to adjust the volume up and down for applications (such as Windows Media Player) or Windows Sounds (such as the little sounds you hear when you get an error message or take certain actions in Windows).

* **Balance slider:** If you have a stereo device, use this slider to adjust sound between right and left speakers. (The Balance slider is not shown in Figure 14-5.)

* **Mute buttons:** To mute a device, click the Mute button; a small red circle with a line through the middle appears next to the Mute button (see Figure 14-6).

3. Click the Close button and then click OK to close the Volume Mixer dialog box.

 A handy shortcut exists for adjusting the volume of your default sound devices. Click the Volume button (which looks like a little gray speaker) on the right side of the Windows Vista taskbar. Use the slider on the Volume pop-up that appears to adjust the volume or, if you want, click the Mute button to turn sounds off.

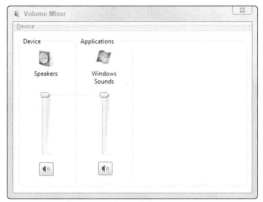

Figure 14-5: The Master Volume dialog box

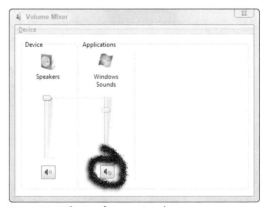

Figure 14-6: The Mute feature activated

Adjust Your Sound Scheme

1. Choose Start⇨Control Panel⇨Hardware and Sound.

2. In the resulting Hardware and Sound window, as shown in Figure 14-7, click the Change System Sounds link.

3. In the Sound dialog box that appears, click to display the Sounds tab, if it's not already displayed (see Figure 14-8).

4. Click to display the Sound Scheme drop-down list and choose the sound scheme you prefer:

   • **Windows Default** uses the sound scheme that came installed with Windows Vista.

   • **No Sounds** turns off all sounds associated with Windows events.

5. Click OK to save the new settings.

 If you want to change individual sounds associated with Windows events, such as exiting Windows, you can click an individual event in the Program list and then choose a new setting from the Sounds drop-down list. You can also click Browse to display the Browse for New Sound dialog box. When you finish, click the Save As button to save the new Sound Scheme.

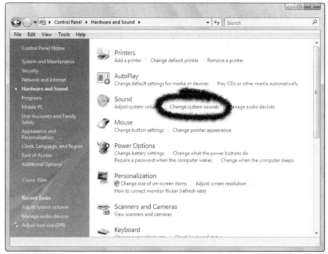

Figure 14-7: The Hardware and Sound window

Figure 14-8: The Sounds tab of the Sound dialog box

Download a Sound File

1. Depending on how the Web site you're visiting has set things up, you do one of the following actions to download a sound file:

   - Click a download button or link and follow the instructions for selecting a destination location on your hard drive to download the file to.

   - Click the sound file link and choose Save. In the Save As dialog box that appears (see Figure 14-9), use the Save In drop-down list to locate a place to save the file, enter a File Name, and click Save. A dialog box shows the download progress; when it's completed, click the Open button. A player that the sound file is associated with, such as MusicMatch Jukebox or Windows Media Player, opens and plays the file.

   - Click the sound file link, and a download dialog box opens. Follow the steps in the previous option to select a download location, name the file, and proceed with the download.

2. When the file finishes downloading, it might open and play automatically in a media player, such as Windows Media Player, as shown in Figure 14-10. If it doesn't, you have to take one of the following actions:

   - You can locate the saved file by using Windows Explorer; then double-click the file to play it.

   - One final option is to open Windows Media Player, choose File⇨Open, locate the file, and open it. Then use the player's tools to play the file.

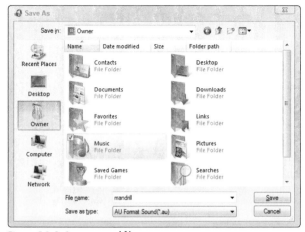

Figure 14-9: Saving a sound file

Figure 14-10: A downloaded file opened in Windows Media Player

Play Music with Windows Media Player

1. To open Windows Media Player and begin working with music files, choose Start➪All Programs➪ Windows Media Player.

2. Click the Maximize button in the resulting Media Player window. (Maximize is in the upper-right corner of the window, next to the X-shaped Close button, sporting two square icons.)

3. Click the arrow on the bottom of the Library button at the top of the window and click Music.

4. In the window listing music files that appears, click the Library folder that contains the music you want to play (as shown in Figure 14-11).

5. Double-click a file to begin the playback (see Figure 14-12). Use tools at the bottom of the screen to do the following:

   - Adjust the volume by clicking and dragging the slider left (to make it softer) or right (to make it louder). Click the megaphone-shaped volume icon to mute the sound (and click it again to turn the sound back on).

   - Pause the playback by clicking the round Pause button in the center of the toolbar.

   - Stop the playback by clicking the square-shaped Stop button toward the left.

   - Skip to the next or previous track by clicking the arrow buttons to the left or right of the Pause button.

6. Click the Close button to close Media Player.

Figure 14-11: The Library folder containing videos for playback

Figure 14-12: The video playback window

Create a Playlist

1. Choose Start⇨Windows Media Player. (If Windows Media Player doesn't appear on your main Start menu, choose All Programs⇨Accessories to locate it.)

2. Click the Create Playlist link. The field opens for editing with the words New Playlist displayed (see Figure 14-13).

3. Enter a name for the playlist and press Enter. The Playlist panel appears on the right.

4. Locate the sound files you want to place in the playlist and click and drag them to the Playlist panel.

5. Click the Save Playlist button (see Figure 14-14). The playlist appears under Playlists in the left pane. When you click the playlist, all titles in the playlist appear in the list on the right. Double-click any item in the playlist to play it.

 You can rename or delete a playlist. Right-click the list under the Playlists category in the left pane and then choose Rename or Delete, respectively.

Figure 14-13: A new blank playlist

Figure 14-14: Saving a playlist

Listen to Online Radio

1. With Windows Media Player open, click the Media Guide tab. The WindowsMedia.com page appears (see Figure 14-15).

2. Click on the Internet Radio link and then click on a featured station. You can also click on the right-facing arrow sign next to a music category such as Top 40 to locate a station.

3. Click the arrow to the left of a station to display additional information about it (see Figure 4-16).

4. Click the station you want to listen to and then click the Play link; the station plays. You can use the controls at the bottom left of the screen to stop, pause, play, or move forward or backward in the radio programming.

5. When you are done listening, click the Close button in Windows Media Player to close it.

 Some radio stations require that you pay for a subscription so it will cost you to get your music. One cue to a station that asks that you pay are the words "Try it free today," which suggests tomorrow may not be!

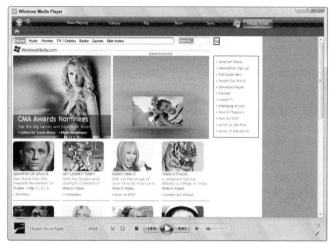

Figure 14-15: The WindowsMedia.com page

Figure 14-16: Stations in the Jazz category

Record with Windows Sound Recorder

1. Attach a microphone to your computer. (See your computer manual for how to do this.)

2. Choose Start⇨All Programs⇨Accessories⇨ Entertainment⇨Sound Recorder.

3. In the resulting Sound Recorder window (see Figure 14-17), click the Start Recording button.

4. The Position and Length boxes begin to record the number of seconds of your recording, and the slider begins to move to the right. Click the Stop Recording button shown in Figure 14-18 to stop the recording. The Save As dialog box appears. Enter a File name and click the Save button.

5. To play back the recording, locate the file you saved and double-click it. Windows Media Player opens, playing the file.

6. Click Close to close the Windows Media Player window.

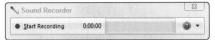

Figure 14-17: The Sound Recorder window ready to record

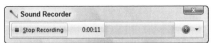

Figure 14-18: A recording in progress

 While playing back a recording, you can rewind or fast forward either by clicking and dragging the slider bar backward or forward or by clicking the Rewind button (two left-facing arrows) or the Forward button (two right-facing arrows).

Working with Printers, Faxes, and Scanners

A computer is a great storehouse for data, images, and other digital information, but sometimes you need ways to turn printed documents into electronic files you can work with on your computer, or print *hard copies* (a fancy term for paper printouts) of electronic documents and images. Here are a few key ways to do just that:

➡ **Printers** allow you to create hard copies of your files on paper, transparencies, or whatever stock your printer can accommodate. To use a printer, you have to have software installed — a *print driver* — and use certain settings to tell your computer how to find the printer and what to print.

➡ You use a **scanner** to create electronic files — pictures, essentially — from hard copies of documents, pictures, or whatever will fit into/onto your scanner. You can then work with the files, fax or e-mail them, or print them. Scanners also require that you install a driver that comes with your machine.

➡ **Fax machines** let you send an electronic version of documents over your dial-up (phone line), broadband, or wireless Internet connection. The image received on the other end is an electronic version. For some fax machines, to use them you insert a hard copy, enter a phone number, and send it on its way. However, if your computer is connected to the Internet, you can also fax an electronic document directly from your computer using a built-in feature in Windows Vista. Depending on your recipient's fax machine setup, either a printed fax or electronic file will be received.

Chapter 15

Get ready to . . .

Install a Printer

1. A printer driver is the software your computer needs in order to communicate with your printer. After plugging your printer into your computer, read and follow the instructions that came with the printer. Some printers require that you install software before connecting them, but others can be connected right away.

2. Turn on your computer and then follow the option that fits your needs:

   • **If your printer is a Plug and Play device,** Windows will be able to detect it and install the appropriate driver without you doing a thing. Connect the printer to your computer using the appropriate cable; Windows installs what it needs automatically and you're done with this step list.

   • **If your printer came with a disc,** insert the CD or DVD into the drive and follow the on-screen instructions. When you finish the instructions, your printer should be installed and ready to use, and you're done with this step list.

   • **If neither of the preceding bullets applies to you,** choose Start➪Control Panel➪Printer; in the Printers window that appears, click Add a Printer to start the Add Printer Wizard. If this is the option that you're following, proceed to the next step in this list.

3. If you choose the third option in Step 2, in the Add Printer Wizard, select the Add a Local Printer option (see Figure 15-1). Click Next.

4. In the resulting wizard screen (the Choose a Printer Port screen, as shown in Figure 15-2), you need to specify which slot (called a port) on your computer you

Figure 15-1: Click on Add a Local Printer

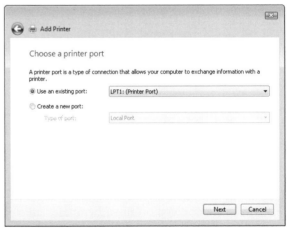

Figure 15-2: The default port is usually the correct setting

plugged your printer into. Click the down arrow on the Use an Existing Port field and select a port. It's probably safe just to use the recommended port setting that Windows selects for you. Click Next.

5. In the next wizard screen (the Install the Printer Driver screen; see Figure 15-3), choose the manufacturer of your printer and then choose a printer. Click Next.

6. In the resulting Type a Printer Name screen (see Figure 15-4), enter a printer name. If you don't want this to be your default printer (the one your computer automatically selects to print), deselect the Set As the Default Printer option. Click Next.

7. In the resulting screen, click Finish to complete the Add Printer Wizard.

 You can install as many printers as you like. For example, you might have a color laser printer for higher end jobs and a less high quality deskjet for everyday printing. Whichever printer you use most often should be your default so you don't have to select it every time you print. See the task later in this chapter titled Make A Printer the Default for more about how to do this.

Figure 15-3: The Install the Printer Driver screen

Figure 15-4: Naming the printer

Set Printer Preferences

1. Your printer might have capabilities such as being able to print in color or black and white, or print in draft quality (which uses less ink) or high quality (which produces a darker, crisper image). To modify these settings for all documents you print, choose Start⇨Control Panel⇨Printer (in the Hardware and Sound group).

2. In the resulting Printers window, any printers you have installed are listed. Click a printer to select it and then click the Select Printing Preferences link.

3. In the Printing Preferences dialog box that appears (as shown in Figure 15-5), click any of the tabs to display various settings, such as Color (see Figure 15-6). Note that different printers might display different choices and different tabs in this dialog box.

4. Click OK to close the dialog box and save settings and then click the Close button to close other open Control Panel windows.

Figure 15-5: The Printing Preferences dialog box

Figure 15-6: The Color tab

Print a File

1. When you have your printer all set up and you're ready to print a file, first open the file in the application in which it was created. (You can find the steps for starting a program in Chapter 11 and for opening files in Chapter 10.)

2. Choose File⇨Print. Note that if you're working with a Microsoft Office 2007 program, the procedure to print involves clicking the Microsoft Office button and then choosing Print.

3. In the resulting Print dialog box (see Figure 15-7), select what to print from the Page Range section. The options in this dialog box might vary but generally include the following:

   - **All** prints all pages in the document.

   - **Current Page** prints whatever page your cursor is active in at the moment.

   - **Selection** prints any text or objects that you have selected within the file when you choose the Print command.

   - **Pages** prints a page range (two numbers separated by a hyphen) and/or series of pages (different page numbers separated by commas) that you enter in the field. For example, enter 3–11 to print pages 3 through 11; or enter 3, 7, 10–12 to print pages 3, 7, and 10 through 12.

4. In the Number of Copies field, click the up or down arrow to set the number of copies to make; if you want multiple copies collated (printed in page order), select the Collate check box.

5. Click OK to proceed with printing.

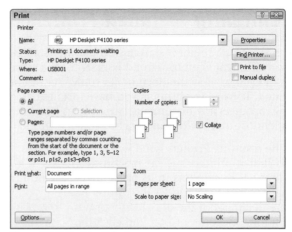

Figure 15-7: The Print dialog box

 You can use the Page Setup dialog box prior to printing to specify settings such as printing in landscape or portrait orientation (that is, with the long side of the paper across the top of your document or along the side); modify the document margins (how much white space to leave around the edge of the document); or print headers or footers (text you want to appear either on the top or bottom of every page, such as a page number or document title. To make these settings, choose File⇨Page Setup to display the Page Setup dialog box.

 Different applications might offer different options in the Print dialog box. For example, PowerPoint offers several options for what to print, including slides, handouts, and the presentation outline, and Outlook allows you to print e-mails in table or in memo style.

View Currently Installed Printers

1. Over time, you might install multiple printers, in which case you might want to remind yourself of the capabilities of each or view the documents you've sent to be printed. To view the printers you have installed and view or cancel any documents currently in line for printing, choose Start⇨Control Panel⇨Printer.

2. In the resulting Printers window (see Figure 15-8), a list of installed printers and fax machines appears. If a printer has documents in its print queue, the number of documents is listed under the printer name. If you want more detail about the documents or want to cancel a print job, select the printer and click the See What's Printing button. In the window that appears, you can click a document and choose Document⇨Cancel to stop the printing, if you want. Click the Close button to return to the Printers window.

3. You can right-click any printer and then choose Properties to see details about it (see Figure 15-9), such as which port it's plugged into or whether it can print color copies.

4. Click the Close button (the red X in the upper-right corner) to close the window.

 When you click a printer in the list, a list of Printer Tasks appears to the left. You can use links in this list to view current print jobs for that printer, pause printing in progress, or set printer properties. See the task "Set Printer Preferences," earlier in this chapter, for more about this last procedure.

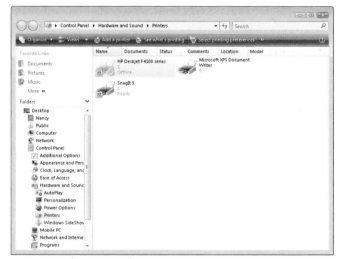

Figure 15-8: The Printers window

Figure 15-9: The Properties dialog box for a printer

Make a Printer the Default

1. If you install a new printer, you might want to make it the default printer so it's always used, unless you specify otherwise when printing a document. To make a printer the default, choose Start➪Control Panel➪Printer (in the Hardware and Sound group).

2. In the resulting Printers window (as shown in Figure 15-10), the current default printer is indicated by a check mark.

3. Click any printer that isn't set as the default and click the Set as Default button, which appears at the top of the window, as shown in Figure 15-11. (If you click the printer that is already set as the default, the Set as Default command isn't available.)

4. Click the Close button in the Printers window to save the new settings and exit the window.

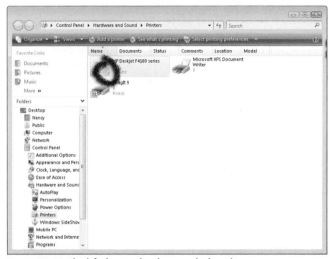

Figure 15-10: The default printer has the green check mark

Figure 15-11: Click Set as Default

Remove a Printer

1. Over time, you might upgrade to a new printer and toss the old one. When you do, you might want to also remove the older printer driver from your computer so your Printers window isn't cluttered with printers you don't need anymore. To remove a printer, choose Start⇨Control Panel⇨Printer (in the Hardware and Sound group).

2. In the resulting Printers window (see Figure 15-12), click a printer to choose it.

3. Click the Delete This Printer button on the toolbar. (If this command isn't visible, click the double-arrow icon on the right side to see more commands.)

4. In the Printers dialog box that appears, click Yes; the Printers window closes, and your printer is removed from the printer list.

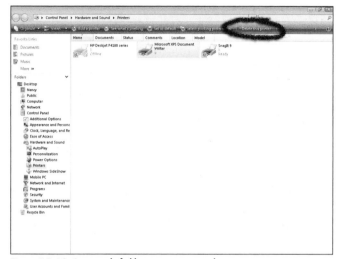

Figure 15-12: Getting rid of old printers to remove clutter

 If you remove a printer, it's removed from the list of installed printers, and if it was the default printer, Windows makes another printer you have installed the default printer. You can no longer print to the deleted printer unless you install it again. See the task, "Install a Printer," if you decide you want to use that printer again.

Rename a Printer

1. Choose Start➪Control Panel and click the Printers link under the Hardware and Sound category.

2. In the resulting Printers window, right-click a printer in the list and choose Rename.

3. The printer name is now available to edit (see Figure 15-13); type a new name and then click outside the printer to save the new name.

4. Click the Close button to close the Printers window.

 Renaming printers can come in handy, especially if you have set up a computer network and various people access different on it. For example, name your two printers Color Printer in Den and B&W Printer in Basement and there will be no doubt where your document will be printing to!

Figure 15-13: The Printer window

Install a Scanner

1. Before you can scan documents into your computer with a scanner, you need to install the scanner driver so your scanner and computer can communicate. Start by connecting the scanner to your computer's USB or parallel port (a slot on your computer you plug a cable into as shown in Figure 15-13), depending on your scanner connection (see your scanner manual for information about how it connects to your computer).

2. Some scanners use Plug and Play, a technology that Windows uses to recognize equipment and automatically install and set it up. If your scanner is Plug and Play enabled, Windows Vista shows a Found New Hardware message in the Task Bar notification area (in the lower-right corner). Most Plug and Play devices will then automatically install; the message changes to verify the installation is complete, and that's all you have to do. If that doesn't happen, you're not using a Plug and Play device, so you should click the Found New Hardware message to proceed.

3. In the resulting Found New Hardware Wizard (this starts only if you don't permit Windows Vista to automatically connect to Windows Update), click Yes, This Time Only, and then click Next.

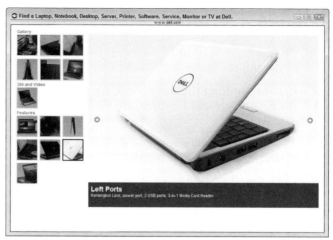

Figure 15-14: USB ports

To be sure your hardware is compatible with Windows Vista check your manufacturer's specifications on their Web site, or visit this Microsoft site for advice: `http://technet.microsoft.com/en-us/windows/aa905090.aspx`.

4. If you have an installation CD for the scanner, insert it in your CD drive and click Next. Windows Vista searches for your scanner driver software and installs it.

5. Choose Start⇨Control Panel⇨Hardware and Sound⇨Scanners and Cameras.

6. In the resulting Scanners and Camera dialog box, click the Add Device button.

7. In the resulting Scanner and Camera Installation Wizard, click Next. In the next screen of the wizard (see Figure 15-15), click a Manufacturer in the list on the left and then click a model in the list on the right.

8. Follow the wizard directions based on the model of scanner you choose in Step 6 and whether you have a manufacturer's disc (a CD- or DVD-ROM). If you don't have a disc, Windows will help you download software from the Internet. When you reach the end of the wizard, click Finish to complete the installation.

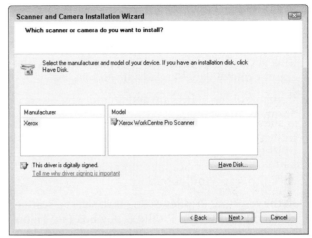

Figure 15-15: Selecting your scanner

Modify Scanner Settings

1. After you install a scanner, you might want to take a look at or change its default settings. To do so, choose Start➪Control Panel➪Hardware and Sound.

2. In the resulting Hardware and Sound window, click Scanners and Cameras.

3. In the resulting Scanners and Cameras dialog box, a list of installed scanners appears (see Figure 15-16). Click any scanner in the Scanners and Cameras area and then click the Scan Profiles button.

4. In the resulting Profiles dialog box, select a scanner and click Edit. In the Edit Profile dialog box (see Figure 15-17), review the settings, which might include (depending on your scanner model) color management for fine-tuning the way colors are scanned and resolution settings that control how detailed a scan is performed. (The higher the resolution is, the crisper and cleaner your electronic document will be, but the more time it might take to scan.)

5. Click Save Profile to return to the Properties dialog box and then click the Close button twice to close the Edit Profiles and Scanners and Cameras dialog boxes.

 When you're ready to run a scan, place the item to be scanned in your scanner. Depending on your model, you may place the item on a flat "bed" with a hinged cover or you may feed it through a tray. Check your scanner manual for the specific procedure to initiate a scan (for example, pressing a Scan or Start button). After you begin the scan, your computer automatically detects it and displays a dialog box showing you the scan progress and allowing you to view and save the scanned item.

Figure 15-16: The Scanners and Cameras dialog box

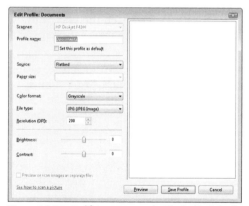

Figure 15-17: Modifying settings in the Edit Profile dialog box

Set Up a Fax

1. After you've connected a fax machine to your computer, if you want to modify the machine's settings, choose Start⇨Control Panel⇨Printer (in the Hardware and Sound group).

2. In the resulting Printers window, as shown in Figure 15-18, click a fax in the list and then click the Select Printing Preferences button.

3. In the Fax Printing Preferences dialog box that appears (see Figure 15-19), make any of the following settings. *Note:* These settings might vary slightly, depending on your fax model.

    *   The default paper size is probably fine for more of your faxes, but if not, click the arrow for the Paper Size drop-down list and choose another paper size. Alternatively, type standard paper dimensions in the two fields below, such as 8 ½ x 14 for legal size paper.

    *   On the right, under the Click for Orientation label, you can click the image to change orientation between landscape and portrait. Landscape prints with the long side of the paper across the top and portrait prints with the long side of the paper along the side.

    *   Make settings for image quality, if available, to specify how high quality a printing setting you want. (My fax, shown in Figure 15-18, doesn't have this setting.)

4. Click OK to close the dialog box and then click OK to close the Printers window.

Figure 15-18: Choose your fax in this window

Figure 15-19: Set up fax properties here

Send a Fax

1. To send a fax, you use the Print dialog box. With an application open, choose File (or the Microsoft Office button in Office 2007 products)⇨Print.

2. In the Print dialog box that appears (see Figure 15-20), click the arrow on the Name drop-down list and select your fax device or program.

   If you chose not to change any default settings after installing your fax (as explained in the previous task), the Fax Setup Wizard might appear. Click the Connect to a Fax Modem link and then follow instructions to set up the connection.

3. When you finish the setup wizard, a new fax cover page form is displayed (see Figure 15-21).

4. Enter the recipient's information (this must be a contact you have saved with a fax number) and subject, as well as any message you want to include.

5. Click the Send button on the toolbar to send the fax.

 If you have a scanner, you can scan images into your computer and then send them as attachments to an e-mail, which is covered in Chapter 18. If the person you're trying to communicate with can't receive a fax, consider this alternative.

Figure 15-20: Choosing to print to a fax machine

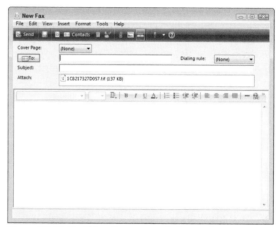

Figure 15-21: Modifying the cover page before sending

Part IV
Going Online

The 5th Wave   By Rich Tennant

"Since we got it, he hasn't moved from that spot for eleven straight days. Oddly enough they call this 'getting up and running' on the internet."

Internet Basics

For many people, going online might be the major reason to buy a computer. You can use the Internet to check stock quotes, play interactive games with others, and file your taxes, for example. The Internet can provide wonderful ways to keep in touch with family and friends located around the country or on the other side of the world via e-mail or instant messaging. You can share photos or connect with others who share your hobbies or interests.

But before you begin all those wonderful activities, it helps to understand some basics about the Internet and how it works and to master the art of getting around the online environment.

This chapter helps you to set up an Internet connection, discover how to browse the Web, search for the information you need, and organize your online experience for ease of use using the Favorites feature. Finally, you learn how to download files so you can buy software, music, movies, and more all from your computer, to use Content Advisor to avoid unsavory sites, and to print the contents of a Web page.

Chapter 16

Get ready to . . .

Set Up Your Internet Connection

1. Today it makes sense to use a broadband connection if you're planning on connecting to the Internet on a regular basis and can afford the monthly fee. To set up your computer for broadband access, you can start by choosing Start➪Network.

2. In the resulting window, click Network and Sharing Center.

3. In the resulting Network and Sharing Center window (see Figure 16-1), click the Set Up a Connection or Network link.

4. In the Choose a Connection dialog box, accept the default option Connect to the Internet by clicking Next.

5. In the resulting dialog box, click your connection type. (These steps follow the selection of Broadband.) If you have a current connection, a window appears and asks whether you want to use a current connection. Click Set Up a New Connection.

6. In the resulting dialog box, shown in Figure 16-2, enter the username and password your Internet Service Provider (ISP) gave you, enter a connection name of your choosing (if you want to assign one), and then click Connect. Windows automatically detects the connection, and the Network and Sharing Center window appears with your connection listed.

7. Click the Close button to close the dialog box.

 In many cases, if you have a CD from your ISP, you don't need to follow the preceding steps. Just pop that CD into your CD-ROM drive, and instructions for setting up your account appear.

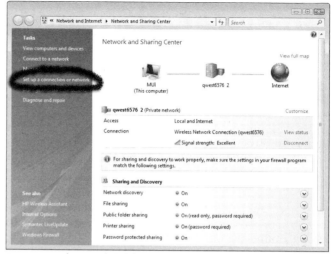

Figure 16-1: The Network and Sharing Center window

Figure 16-2: The Connect to the Internet dialog box

Disconnect an Internet Connection

1. Choose Start➪Control Panel.

2. In the Control Panel window, click the Network and Internet link.

3. In the Network and Internet window (refer to Figure 16-3), click the Connect to a Network link.

4. In the resulting Connect to a Network dialog box (see Figure 16-4), click on the active connection and then click the Disconnect button.

5. Click the Close button to close the dialog box.

 If you have a Network icon displayed in the Notification Area of the taskbar, you can right-click and choose Disconnect from and click on the active connection you want to disconnect.

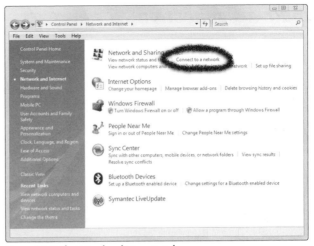

Figure 16-3: The Network and Internet window

Figure 16-4: The Connect to a Network dialog box

Repair a Connection

1. Choose Start➪Network.

2. In the Network window, click the Network and Sharing Center link.

3. In the Network and Sharing Center window, click Diagnose and Repair.

4. A progress window appears telling you that Windows is checking your connection (see Figure 16-5).

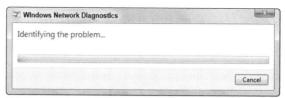

Figure 16-5: The Network Diagnostics window

 Sometimes repairing a connection doesn't do the trick. In that case, it's best to delete the connection and just create it again by clicking the Create a New Connection link in the Network Connections window and then entering the correct settings.

Navigate the Web

1. After you've connected to the Internet, you're ready to step foot into the virtual world. The first thing you should know is how to navigate the Web by using a browser. Internet Explorer (also called simply IE) from Microsoft is probably built into your Windows-based computer, so it's a good place to start. Open Internet Explorer by clicking its icon on the Quick Launch bar located on the Windows Vista taskbar.

2. Enter a Web site address in the Address bar, as shown in Figure 16-6, and then press Enter. If you don't know any URLs, just type **www.understandingnano.com** to visit one of my Web sites.

3. On the resulting Web site, you'll notice different areas of content on the page, including a navigation bar that includes text or graphics you can click to visit various pages on the site, as well as content in the form of text and graphics. Usually, the browser window doesn't display a whole page. To display the rest of the page, click the arrow at the bottom of the scroll bar on the right side of the window scroll down the page. Or press the Page Down key on your keyboard.

 The Refresh and Stop buttons on the right end of the Address bar are useful for navigating sites. Click Refresh to redisplay the current page. This is especially useful if a page updates information frequently (such as on a stock market site) or if a page doesn't load correctly; it might load correctly when refreshed. If you made a mistake entering the address or if the page is taking longer than you'd like to load, click Stop to halt the process.

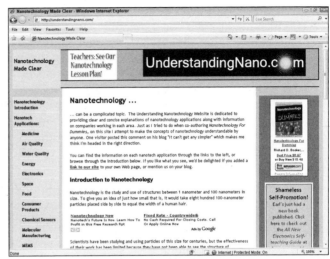

Figure 16-6: Entering an address in the address bar

4. When you want to go somewhere else, either click a link (which might jump you to another page on the current site or to another site) or enter another address in the address bar to jump to a different site. Note that you can also use tab features in many browsers to open multiple sites on different tabs. See the next task for more about tabs.

5. Click the Back button to move back to the previous page that you visited. Click the Forward button to go forward to the page that you visited before you clicked the Back button.

6. Click the down-pointing arrow at the far right of the address bar to display a list of sites that you visited recently, as shown in Figure 16-7. Click a site in this list to go there.

 A *pop-up* is a small window that might open from time to time as you browse the Web, and it contains annoying advertisements. You can use the Pop-Up Blocker to stop pop-up ads from appearing. Choose Tools⇨Pop-Up Blocker⇨Turn On Pop-Up Blocker to activate this feature. You can also use the Pop-Up Blocker Settings command on this same menu to specify sites on which you want to allow pop-ups. For details, see Chapter 17, which explains how you set privacy settings.

Figure 16-7: Choosing a site from your browser history list

Use Tabs in Internet Explorer

Internet Explorer (IE) and several other browsing programs, such as Opera, offer a feature called tabbed browsing. In addition to opening multiple home pages on tabs, you can open new tabs as you browse the Web (see Figure 16-8). You can then click tabs to jump to other sites you have displayed on those tabs without having to navigate backwards or forwards in a single window to sites you've previously visited.

Here's how to use tabbed browsing for maximum efficiency in Internet Explorer:

➡ Click the New Tab button (this is the small tab to the right of any open tabs with a small page icon on it) to open a new, blank tab. The new tab now appears above the body of the tab area to the right of any other open tabs. Enter an address in the address bar and press Enter; the site appears in your newly displayed tab.

➡ Click another tab to jump to another site.

➡ Click the New Tab button again to add another tab for browsing.

➡ Click the Close button on any active tab to close it.

 You can open a linked page in a new tab quickly by right-clicking the link and choosing Open in New Tab. A new tab opens with the page displayed.

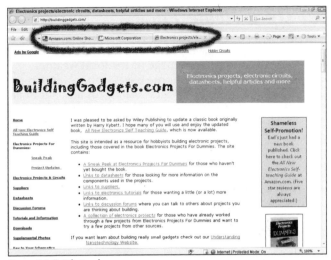

Figure 16-8: Tabs in a browser

Set Up a Home Page

1. If you find yourself going to one page often — for example, your e-mail page or the local weather — you can set one or more home pages. Whenever you open your browser, home pages display on tabs automatically. Open IE and choose Tools➪Internet Options.

2. In the resulting Internet Options dialog box, on the General tab, enter a Web site address to use as your home page, as shown in Figure 16-9. Note that you can enter multiple home pages that will appear on different tabs every time you open IE. Alternatively, click one of the following preset option buttons, as shown in Figure 16-9:

   - **Use Current:** Sets whatever page is currently displayed in the browser window as your home page.

   - **Use Default:** This setting makes the MSN Web page your home page.

   - **Use Blank:** If you're a minimalist, this setting is for you. No Web page displays; you just see a blank area.

3. Click OK to save your setting and close the dialog box.

4. Back in Internet Explorer, click the Home icon (it looks like a house) to go to your home page.

 If you want to have more than one home page, you can create multiple home page tabs that will display when you click the Home icon. Click the arrow next to the Home icon and choose Add or Change Home Page. In the Add or Change Home Page dialog box that appears, select Add This Webpage to Your Home Page Tabs radio button and then click Yes. Display other sites and repeat this procedure for all the home page tabs you want.

Figure 16-9: The Internet Options dialog box

 To remove a home page you have set up, click the arrow next to the Home icon and choose Remove. In the submenu that appears, choose a particular home page or choose Remove All.

Search the Web

1. Simple-to-use programs called *search engines* make it easy to find information on the Internet — probably more information than you ever wanted! To use Internet Explorer's search feature, open IE and click in the Search text box in the top-right corner on the toolbar. The default search engine is Windows Live Search.

2. Enter a search term in the text box and then click Search. A *search term* is simply a word or phrase that relates to the results you seek. For example, if you want information about astronomy, enter the word **astronomy** or the phrase **black holes** and then press Enter.

3. In the resulting list of links (see Figure 16-10), click a link to go that Web page.

4. If you don't see the link that you need, click and drag the scrollbar downward to view more results.

 Note that browsers often return sponsored links at the top or side of the search results page. These are sites that pay to have their information included. You can click them, but remember that they are paid advertisers, and there's a greater risk of downloading dangerous software to your computer if you click a sponsored link.

Figure 16-10: Search results in a browser

 Knowing how search engines work can save you time. For example, if you search by entering *golden retriever*, you typically get sites that contain both words or either word. If you put a plus sign between these two keywords, *golden+retriever*, you get only sites that contain both words.

Find Content on a Web Page

1. With IE open and the Web page that you want to search displayed, choose Edit⇨Find On This Page.

2. In the resulting dialog box, as shown in Figure 16-11, enter the word that you want to search for. Use the following options to narrow your results:

   - **Match Whole Word Only:** Select this option if you want to find only the whole word (for example, if you enter **cat** and want to find only *cat* and not *catatonic* or *catastrophe*).

   - **Match Case:** Select this option if you want to match the case (for example, if you enter **Catholic** and want to find only the always-capitalized religion and not the adjective *catholic*).

3. In the Direction area, select Up if you want to search the beginning of the page first; select Down if you want the end of the page to be searched first.

4. Click the Find Next button. The first instance of the word is highlighted on the page (see Figure 16-12). If you want to find another instance, click the Find Next button again.

5. When you're done searching, click the Close button in the Find dialog box.

 Many Web sites, such as www.amazon.com, have a Search feature that allows you to search not only the displayed Web page but all Web pages on the Web site. Look for a Search text box or link and make sure that it searches the site and not the entire Internet.

Figure 16-11: The Find dialog box

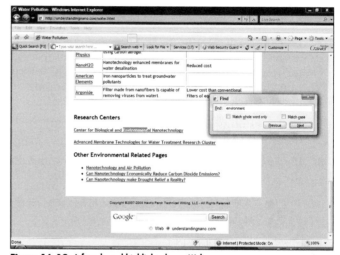

Figure 16-12: A found word highlighted on a Web page

View Your Browsing History

1. Choose View➪Explorer Bar➪History to display sites you've visited previously.

2. In the resulting History pane, click the arrow on the View button to show all viewing options. (The default view is By Date.)

3. With By Date view selected (as shown in Figure 16-13), click one of the folders in the list to display all sites in a particular time period, such as Last Week or 2 Weeks Ago. If you want to revisit a site in the list, click it, and you're there.

 To clear the IE History feature, choose Tools➪Internet Options. On the General tab, click the Clear History button. To change how many days of searching the History feature saves, on the General tab, change the Days to Keep Pages in History setting by clicking the up or down spinner arrow. You can also delete a single site or folder from the History pane by right-clicking it and choosing Delete.

 You can quickly add a site you view in the History pane to your Favorites. Right-click on the site in the History pane and choose Add to Favorites. That's it!

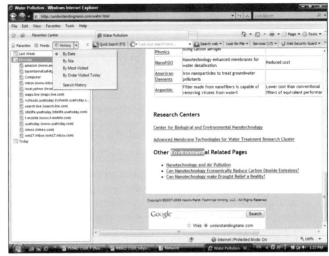

Figure 16-13: The History pane

Add a Web Site to Favorites

1. Open IE, enter the URL of a Web site that you want to add to your Favorites list, and then press Enter.

2. Click the Add to Favorites button and then choose Add to Favorites.

3. In the resulting Add a Favorite dialog box, as shown in Figure 16-14, modify the name of the Favorite listing to something easily recognizable.

4. If you want, choose another folder to store the favorite in by clicking the arrow on the Create In field. You can also create a folder to store the favorite in by clicking the New Folder button, entering the folder name in the Create a Folder dialog box that appears, and clicking the Create button. Placing favorites in different folders (such as a Finances folder and a Hobbies folder) helps you organize them and find the favorite you need faster.

5. Click Add to add the site to your Favorites list.

6. When you want to return to the site you've saved as a favorite, click the Favorites Center button and then click the name of the site from the list that's displayed (see Figure 16-15).

 Regularly cleaning out your Favorites list is a good idea — after all, do you really need the sites that you used to plan last year's vacation? With the Favorites Center displayed, right-click any item and then choose Delete or Rename to modify the Favorite listing.

 You can keep the Favorites Center displayed as a side pane in Internet Explorer by displaying it and then clicking the Pin the Favorites Center button (which has a left-facing green arrow on it and is located to the right of the History button).

Figure 16-14: The Add a Favorite dialog box

Figure 16-15: The Favorites list

Organize Favorites

1. As you add favorites, they can become jumbled, and it's helpful to tidy them up into folders or otherwise organize them. With Internet Explorer open, click the Add to Favorites button and then choose Organize Favorites.

2. In the resulting Organize Favorites dialog box (see Figure 16-16), click a favorite and then click the New Folder, Move, Rename, or Delete buttons to organize your favorites.

3. When you finish organizing your Favorites, click Close.

 If you create new folders in the preeceding steps, you have to manually transfer files into those folders. To do this, just display the Favorites Center and click and drag files listed there on top of folders.

 I recommend you go through your Favorites folder a couple of times a year and delete items that are no longer of interest so you don't have to scroll through a huge Favorites list. Trust me, those sites that meant a lot to you when you were doing that research on poison ivy after last summer's camping trip won't mean much come Christmas.

Figure 16-16: The Organize Favorites dialog box

Download Files

1. As you browse the Web, you might find files you want to download, such as music files or movie files you buy from an online store or which are free. Open a Web site that offers files you want to download. Typically Web sites offer a Download button or link that initiates a file download.

2. Click the appropriate link to proceed. Windows Vista might display a dialog box asking your permission to proceed with the download; click Yes.

3. In the resulting File Download dialog box, as shown in Figure 16-17, choose either option:

   • **Click Open or Run (this choice depends on the type of file you are downloading) to download to a temporary folder.** You can run an installation program for software, for example. However, beware: If you run a program directly from the Internet, you might be introducing dangerous viruses to your system. You should buy and follow the software manufacturer's instructions to install and set up an antivirus program such as McAfee or Norton Antivirus to scan files before downloading them.

   • **Click Save to save the file to your hard drive.** In the Save As dialog box, select the folder on your computer or removable storage media (a CD-ROM, for example) where you want to save the file. If you're downloading software, you need to locate the downloaded file and click it to run the installation.

Figure 16-17: The File Download dialog box

 If a particular file will take a long time to download (I've had some big ones take over 20 hours!), you might have to babysit it. If your computer goes into standby, it might pause the download. Check in periodically to keep things moving along.

Change Privacy Settings

1. With IE open, choose Tools⇨Internet Options and click the Privacy tab, as shown in Figure 16-18.

2. Click the slider and drag it up or down to make different levels of security settings.

3. Read the choices and select a setting that suits you. Click OK to save it.

 The default Privacy setting — Medium — is probably a good bet for most people. To restore the default setting, click the Default button in the Internet Options dialog box Privacy sheet or use the slider to move back to Medium.

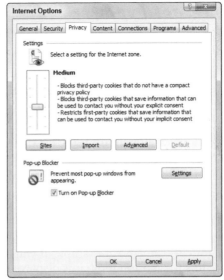

Figure 16-18: The Privacy tab of the Internet Options dialog box

Customize Internet Explorer

1. Open IE.

2. In the resulting home page, customize settings as follows:

- **Select text size.** Choose View⮞Text Size (see Figure 16-19) and select the size text you want displayed.

- **Personalize the Explorer bar.** Choose View⮞ Explorer Bar and click an item from the list that you want to include in the Explorer Bar area on the left side of the IE screen.

- **Add toolbars.** Choose View⮞Toolbars. Try out all the toolbars in the list to see which ones you want to display. (Figure 16-20 shows several toolbars displayed. Note that you can also include any third-party toolbars you might have added. For example, if you run Norton Antivirus the Norton toolbar is displayed, and you can add the Google toolbar to IE by downloading it from www.google.com.)

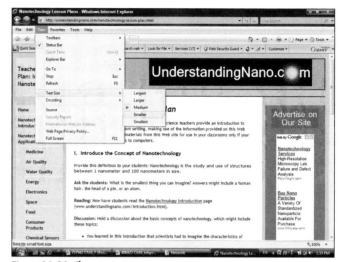

Figure 16-19: Changing text size

 Displaying the History pane in the Explorer bar is useful, but here's a shortcut for visiting recently viewed sites: You can find Web pages that you've visited (up to nine of them) by clicking the arrow to the side of the Back button and choosing one from the list that's displayed.

 You can resize the various panes of Internet Explorer, such as the main Web page view pane and Explorer bar. Move your mouse over the vertical divider between panes until the cursor becomes a line with arrows on both sides; then click and drag the divider to enlarge or shrink a pane.

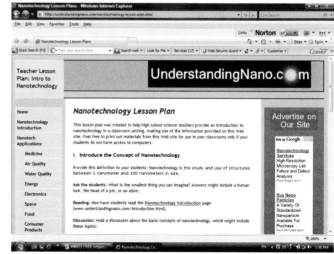

Figure 16-20: Several toolbars displayed

Enable Content Advisor

1. With IE open, choose Tools⇨Internet Options.

2. In the resulting Internet Options dialog box, click the Content tab to display it.

3. Click the Enable button. (*Note:* If there is no Enable button but Disable and Settings buttons instead, Content Advisor is already enabled. Click the Settings button to see the options and make changes if you wish.)

4. On the Ratings tab of the Content Advisor dialog box (see Figure 16-21), click one of the four options: Language, Nudity, Sex, or Violence. Use the slider to set the site-screening level that's appropriate for you.

5. Repeat Step 4 for each of the categories.

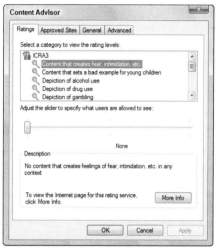

Figure 16-21: The Content Advisor dialog box

6. Click the Approved Sites tab (see Figure 16-22) and enter the name of a specific site that you want to control access to. Then click either of the following options:

   - **Always:** Allows users to view the site, even if it's included in the Content Advisor screening level you've set.

   - **Never:** Means that nobody can visit the site even if it's acceptable to Content Advisor.

7. When you finish making your settings, click OK twice to save them.

 If you want to view sites that you don't want others to see, you can do that, too. On the General tab of the Content Advisor dialog box, make sure that the Supervisor Can Type a Password to Allow Viewers to View Restricted Content check box is selected. Then click Create Password. In the dialog box that appears, enter the password, confirm it, enter a hint, and click OK. Now if you're logged on as the system administrator, you can get to any restricted site by using this password.

Figure 16-22: The Approved Sites tab of the Content Advisor

Print a Web Page

1. If a Web page includes a link or button to print or display a print version of a page, click that and follow the instructions.

2. If the page doesn't include a link for printing, simply press Ctrl+P.

3. In the resulting Print dialog box, decide how much of the document you want to print and click one of the options in the Page Range area, as shown in Figure 16-23.

4. Click the up arrow in the Number of Copies text box to print multiple copies. If you want multiple copies collated, select the Collate check box.

5. Click the Options tab and change settings related to printing frames and links for the page.

6. When you've adjusted all settings, click Print.

 Choosing Current Page or entering page numbers in the Pages text box of the Print dialog box doesn't mean much when printing a Web page; the whole document might print anyway because Web pages aren't divided into pages the way word processor documents are.

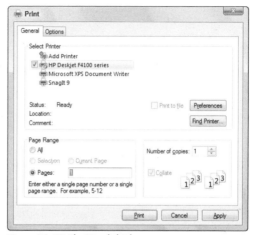

Figure 16-23: The Print dialog box

 Another option for printing a page that doesn't offer a print version link is to right-click anywhere on the page and choose Print from the shortcut menu that appears.

Using E-Mail

*A*n e-mail program is a tool you can use to send text messages to others over the Internet. These messages are delivered to their e-mail *inboxes*, usually within seconds. You can attach files to e-mail and even put graphic images within the message body. You can get an e-mail account through your Internet provider or through sites such as Yahoo! or Microsoft Live Hotmail. These accounts are typically free.

When you have an e-mail account, you can send and receive e-mail through the account provider's e-mail program online, or you can set up a program called an *e-mail client* to access that account on your computer. A couple of well-known e-mail clients are Microsoft Outlook, which comes with Microsoft Office, and Windows Mail, which is built into Windows. These programs typically offer more robust e-mail and contact management features than the programs that providers such as Yahoo! offer.

This chapter takes a look at these tasks:

➠ **Manage your e-mail account.** Set up an e-mail account in Windows Mail and then create, modify, and add rules for your account to operate by.

➠ **Receive, send, and forward messages.** Deal with the ins and outs of receiving and sending e-mail. Use the formatting tools that Windows Mail provides to make your messages pretty.

➠ **Add information into the Address Book.** You can quickly and easily manage your contacts as well as organize the messages you save in e-mail folders.

➠ **Set up the layout of all Windows Mail features.** Add a signature to all messages, create rules for how incoming messages are handled, and send e-mails to large groups in a way that keeps their identities safe.

Chapter
17

Get ready to . . .

Set Up Your E-Mail Account on Windows Mail

1. You can set up Windows Mail to access one or more e-mail accounts so you can manage your mail from one location. Find out from your e-mail account provider what type of account you have (IMAP or POP3, typically) and then follow these steps to set up your account. Choose Start⇨All Programs⇨Windows Mail. In the Windows Mail main window that appears, choose Tools⇨Accounts.

2. In the resulting Internet Accounts dialog box, as shown in Figure 17-1, click Add.

3. In the resulting Internet Connection Wizard (see Figure 17-2), click E-Mail Account and click Next.

4. In the following screen, enter the Display Name that you want to appear on your outgoing e-mails. You might want your full name or initials, for example. Click Next.

 Often email programs allow you to forward e-mail from one account to another. If you have set up one account to forward all messages to another, and you create accounts for both in Windows Mail, you will see both sets of messages. You might consider removing the forwarding setting from the one account now that you are pulling all messages into a central e-mail client.

Figure 17-1: The Internet Accounts dialog box

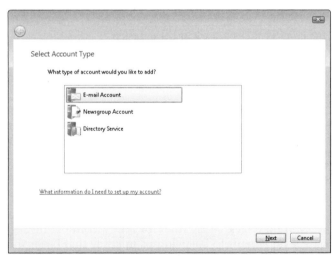

Figure 17-2: The Internet Connection wizard

5. In the Internet E-Mail Address window that appears, enter the e-mail address that you got from your account provider, such as XYZ@aol.com (see Figure 17-3). Click Next.

6. In the Set Up E-Mail Servers window that appears, click the Incoming E-Mail Server Type drop-down list and choose the format: POP3 or IMAP. (Note that though HTTP is still listed, if you select it, Windows Mail tells you it no longer supports HTTP.) If you're not sure about this, check with your e-mail account provider.

7. Enter the Incoming Mail Server and Outgoing Mail Server information in those two fields (see Figure 17-4). Again, you must get this information from your e-mail provider. Click Next.

8. In the Internet Mail Logon window that appears, enter your E-Mail Username and Password in those fields and click Next. In the Congratulations window that appears, click the Finish button to save your account settings and download your e-mail.

Figure 17-3: The Internet E-mail Address window

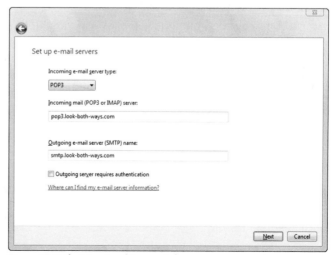

Figure 17-4: The Set-up E-mail Servers window

Manage E-Mail Accounts

1. You can set up more than one e-mail account in Windows Mail (for example, if you and your spouse each have your own account). If you have more than one account, you can choose to make one the default account that Windows Mail will use when you create a new message. You can also decide to delete an old account if you sign up for a different service. Choose Start➪All Programs➪Windows Mail. In the Windows Mail main window that appears, choose Tools➪Accounts.

2. In the resulting Internet Accounts dialog box, select an account on the left (refer to Figure 17-5) and do either of the following:

   • To remove an account, click the Remove button on any of the tabs. A confirming message appears. To delete the account, click Yes.

   • Select an account and click the Set as Default button to make it the account that Windows connects you to when you go online. The word default now appears in parentheses after that account (see Figure 17-6). In the case of the mail server, the default is the one that is used to send any message.

3. Click Close to close the dialog box.

4. When you finish setting up accounts, click the Close button to close the Internet Accounts dialog box.

 The Internet Connection Wizard often requires that you provide certain information about your Internet service provider (ISP), such as its mail server or connection method. Keep this information handy!

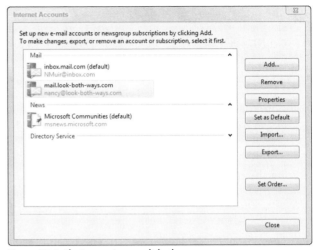

Figure 17-5: The Internet Accounts dialog box

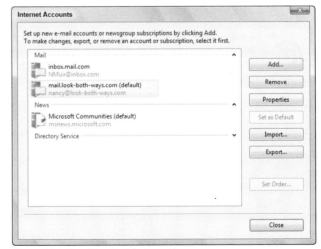

Figure 17-6: Specifying the default e-mail account

Create and Send E-Mail

1. When you want to send a message to somebody else, you open a new e-mail form, address it, enter a subject line and your message, and then send it on its way. Choose Start⇨All Programs⇨Windows Mail.

2. Click the Create Mail button on the Windows Mail toolbar to create a new, blank e-mail form (see Figure 17-7).

3. Type one or more e-mail addresses of the recipient(s) in the To text box. You can also type an address in the Cc text box to send a copy of the message to somebody else.

4. Click in the Subject text box and type a concise yet descriptive subject such as Club Meeting or Holiday Visit.

5. Click in the message text area and type your message (see Figure 17-8).

 E-mail messages may be read in many different programs, such as MSN, Yahoo, and PeoplePC. These programs have different capabilities for displaying text, and what you format and send on its way may not appear quite the same depending on the program used to read it.

 When creating an e-mail, you can address it to a stored address by using the Address Book feature. (See "Add Contacts to the Address Book" later in this chapter.) Just begin to type a stored contact in an address field (To or Cc), and it fills in likely options while you type. When it fills in the correct name, just press Enter to select it.

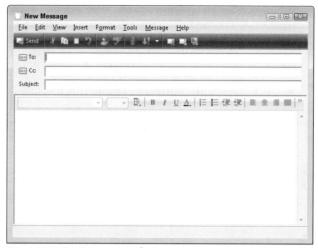

Figure 17-7: Creating a new e-mail message

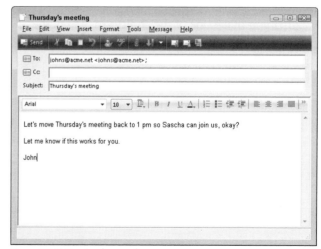

Figure 17-8: Entering the text of your message

6. When you finish typing your message, spell-check it (unless you're the regional state spelling champ). Click the Spelling button; possibly misspelled words get highlighted, and the Spelling dialog box appears (see Figure 17-9). At this point, you have some choices:

- Click the **Ignore button** to ignore this instance of the misspelling.

- Click the **Ignore All button** to ignore all instances.

- Choose a suggested alternative spelling and click the **Change button** to change that instance; or, click the **Change All button** to change all instances of the word. If you wish to enter your own alternate spelling if none of the suggestions are correct, enter the new word in the **Change To** box.

- Click the **Add button** to add the current spelling of the word to the Spelling feature's dictionary so it's never questioned again.

7. After you make one of the choices in Step 6, the Spell Check moves on to the next questionable word, if any, and you can make a new choice. When a window appears telling you the check is complete, click OK to close the Spelling dialog box.

8. Click the Send button. The message is on its way!

 Don't press Enter at the end of a line. Windows Mail has an automatic text wrap feature that bumps the cursor to the next line for you. Also, keep e-mail etiquette in mind as you type. For example, don't type in ALL CAPITAL LETTERS. This is called *shouting*, which is considered rude.

Figure 17-9: Spelling dialog box

 E-mail does involve some etiquette. Do be polite even if you're really, really angry. Your message could be forwarded to just about anybody, just about anywhere, and you don't want to get a reputation as a hothead. Also, be concise because most people don't really like reading long messages on-screen. (It hurts the eyes.) If you have lots to say, consider sending a letter by snail mail (regular mail) or overnight delivery.

 You can also insert a picture in an e-mail. With the e-mail form open, choose Insert⇨Picture. Locate a picture in the Picture window that appears and click Open. The picture fills the background of the e-mail message area.

Format an E-Mail Message

1. Create a new e-mail message or open a message and click Reply or Forward.

2. Select (highlight) the text that you want to format (see Figure 17-10).

3. Use any of the following options to make changes to the font. (See the toolbar containing these tools in Figure 17-10, and a message with various formats applied in Figure 17-11.)

   - **Font drop-down list:** Select an option from this list to apply it to the text.

   - **Font Size drop-down list:** Change the font size here.

   - **Paragraph Style button:** Apply a preset style, such as Heading 1 or Address.

   - **Bold, Italic, or Underline buttons:** Apply styles to selected text.

   - **Font Color button:** Display a color palette and click a color to apply it to selected text.

   - **Formatting Numbers or Formatting Bullets buttons:** Apply numbering order to lists or precede each item with a round bullet.

   - **Align Left, Center, Align Right, or Justify buttons:** Adjust the alignment of the text.

   - **Increase Indentation or Decrease Indentation button:** Indent a paragraph to the right or move it to the left.

   - **Insert Horizontal Line button:** Add a line to your message.

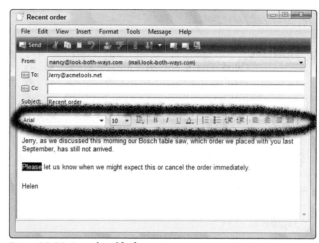

Figure 17-10: Text selected for formatting

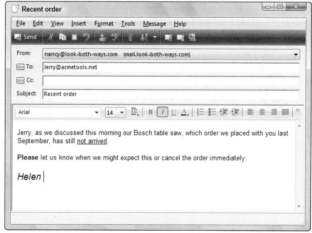

Figure 17-11: A variety of formats applied to an e-mail message

Add Stationery

1. Click the arrow on the Create Mail button in the Windows Mail main window and select a stationery option listed in the menu that appears, or choose the Select Stationery command to get more choices.

2. In the Select Stationery dialog box that appears (see Figure 17-12), select a stationery from the list.

3. Click OK to apply the stationery to the new message.

4. With a new, reply, or forwarded message open, you can also apply stationery by choosing Format➪Apply Stationery and then click a stationery to apply (see Figure 17-13).

 You can edit stationary, for example to add or delete a graphic element. In the Select Stationery dialog box, click on the stationery you want to change and click the Edit button. The stationery opens in a Word document that offers various tools you can use to insert and format text or pictures.

 If you apply stationery and decide that you don't want to use it anymore, just click the arrow on the Create button and select No Stationery from the drop-down list.

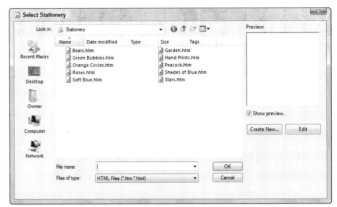

Figure 17-12: The Select Stationery dialog box

Figure 17-13: Selecting stationery from the Format menu in an e-mail message

Read a Message

1. In your Inbox, unread messages sport an icon of an unopened envelope to the left of the message subject. Click an e-mail message in your Inbox or double-click it to open it in a separate window.

2. Use the scrollbars in the message window to scroll down through the message and read it (see Figure 17-14).

3. If the message has an attachment, a paper clip symbol is displayed next to the message in your Inbox; attachments are listed in the Attach box in the open message. To open an attachment, double-click it in the Attach box.

4. In the resulting Mail Attachment dialog box, click the Open button. The attachment opens in whatever program is associated with it (such as the Windows Photo Gallery for a graphics file) or the program it was created in (such as Microsoft Word).

 Instead of opening an attachment, you can save it directly to a removable storage disk or your hard drive. To do so, right-click the attachment name in the Attach field and choose Save As. In the Save As dialog box that appears, choose a location and provide a name for the file; then click Save.

 Warning: E-mail attachments can be dangerous. They might contain viruses or other kinds of malicious software (called *malware*). Never open attachments from somebody you don't know. See Chapter 20 for more information about how to avoid malware.

Figure 17-14: Reading an e-mail message

Reply to a Message

1. Open the message to which you want to reply and then click one of the following buttons, as shown in Figure 17-15:

   - **Reply:** Send the reply to only the author.

   - **Reply All:** Send a reply to the author as well as everyone who received the original message.

2. In the resulting e-mail form, enter any additional recipient(s) in the To and/or Cc text boxes and type your message in the message window area.

3. Click the Send button to send the reply.

 If you don't want to include the original message in your reply, choose Tools➪Options and click the Send tab. Deselect the Include Message in Reply check box and then click OK. Note that when you reply any attachments are not included with the reply.

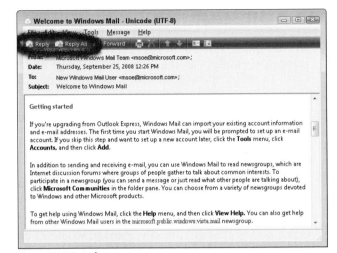

Figure 17-15: Reply options

Send an Attachment

1. You can attach any file to your e-mail to send a document or picture along with your message. Create a new e-mail message, address it, and enter a subject.

2. Click the Attach File to Message button.

3. In the Open dialog box that appears (see Figure 17-16), locate the document or graphics file that you want and then click Open.

4. With the name of the attached file now in the Attach text box (see Figure 17-17), type a message (or not — after all, a picture *is* worth a thousand words).

5. Click the Send button to send.

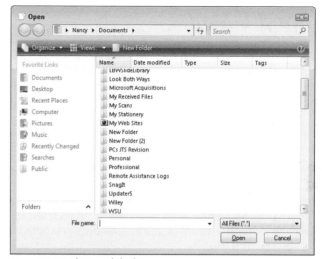

Figure 17-16: The Open dialog box

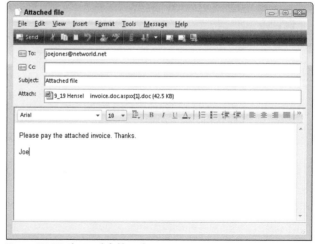

Figure 17-17: The Attach field text box

Forward E-Mail

1. You might get a message that's just too good not to pass on. Passing on, or *forwarding,* e-mail to others is what sends jokes flying around the Internet in droves. Open the e-mail message that you want to forward.

2. Click the Forward button on the toolbar.

3. In the message that appears with Fw added to the beginning of the subject line, enter a new recipient(s) in the To or Cc fields and then enter any message that you want to include in the message window area, as shown in the example in Figure 17-18. If you want to add a BCC (blind carbon copy, invisible to all recipients), click either the To or Cc buttons to display a Select Recipients dialog box.

4. Click Send to forward the message.

 Warning: It's actually dangerous to forward chain mail–type e-mail messages — you know, the ones that say pass this on to ten of your friends. Spammers may end up on those lists of addresses and they may take the entire list of people's e-mail addresses and take advantage of those people in some way. The safest thing if you truly want to forward the contents of such a message is to cut and paste the message into a new message form and address it yourself, putting multiple addresses into the Bcc field rather than the To field so they are invisible to all recipients. You should also make sure there are no list of e-mails within the forwarded message itself to give people's identity away.

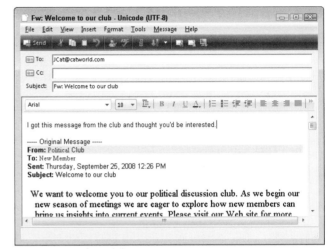

Figure 17-18: A forwarded message.

Create Message Folders

1. Being able to organize the messages you receive and even copies of messages you send is useful. Windows Mail allows you to use existing folders or create new folders that you can move messages into to find them more easily. Choose View⇨Layout to open the Window Layout Properties dialog box.

2. Select check boxes to display the Folders list and Folder bar and then click OK.

3. In the Folders list, click any folder to display its contents.

4. Choose File⇨New⇨Folder (see Figure 17-19).

5. In the resulting Create Folder dialog box (see Figure 17-20), select the folder that you want the new folder to be created in and then enter a new folder name.

6. Click OK.

 Typically, you select the Local Folders item in Step 5 so that the new folder is at the same level as the Inbox, Outbox, and so on. Alternatively, you can select the Inbox item to place the new folder within the Inbox folder.

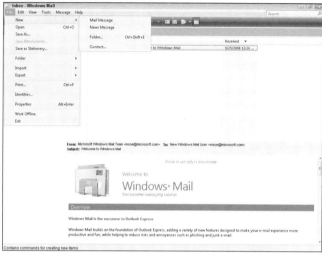

Figure 17-19: Creating a new folder

Figure 17-20: The Create Folder dialog box

Organize Messages in Folders

1. In the Folders list, click a folder to display its contents (see Figure 17-21).

2. To place a message in a folder, you can do one of these actions:

- **Click and drag.** With a folder (such as the Inbox) displayed, click a message and drag it into a folder in the Folders list.

- **Move an open message.** With an e-mail message open, choose File⇨Move to Folder or Copy to Folder. In the Move dialog box that appears (see Figure 17-22), select the appropriate folder and click OK.

- **Move a closed message.** Right-click a message in a displayed folder and choose Move to Folder or Copy to Folder. In the dialog box that appears, select the appropriate folder and click OK.

3. To delete a message, display the folder it's saved in, select the message and then either click the Delete button or press Delete on the keyboard.

 If you try to delete a message from your Deleted Items folder, a message appears asking whether you really want to delete this message permanently. That's because when you delete a message from another folder, it's really not deleted — it's simply placed in the Deleted Items folder. To send it into oblivion, you have to delete it from the Deleted Items folder, confirming your deletion so that Outlook Express is really convinced that you mean what you say.

Figure 17-21: Files in an e-mail folder

Figure 17-22: The Move dialog box

Add Contacts to the Address Book

1. Windows Mail (like most e-mail programs) contains an Address Book feature where you store information about your contacts. Contacts allow you to quickly address e-mail messages using stored e-mail addresses. In the Windows Mail main window, click the Contacts button to open your Contacts window (see Figure 17-23).

2. Double-click a contact to view or edit information.

3. In the resulting Properties dialog box, as shown in Figure 17-24, go to the following tabs to enter contact information:

   • **Name and E-Mail:** Enter the person's name and e-mail address. (This is the only information you must enter to create a contact.)

   • **Home:** Enter the person's home and Web site addresses as well as phone, fax, and cell phone numbers.

   • **Work:** Enter information about the company that the person works for as well as his job title and pager number. You can even add a map to help you find his or her office.

   • **Family:** Enter the person's family members' names, as well as his or her gender, birthday, and anniversary.

   • **Notes:** Enter notes in the form on this tab.

   • **IDs:** Ensure secure communications. *Digital IDs* are certificates that you can use to verify the identity of the person with whom you're communicating. If somebody has provided you with a digital ID, you can store that information here so you can look it up when opening messages from that person.

4. Click OK to save your new contact information and then close the Contacts window.

Figure 17-23: The Contacts window

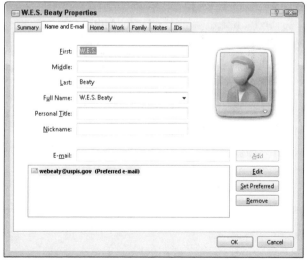

Figure 17-24: The Properties dialog box

Create and Add a Signature

1. Just as you sign a letter *Sincerely yours,* followed by your name, you can add a signature to your e-mail messages. A signature might contain your full name and phone number or even your favorite saying. In Windows Mail, choose Tools➪Options to open the Options dialog box. Click the Signatures tab (see Figure 17-25).

2. Click the New button to create a new signature and then enter your Signatures text.

3. Select the Add Signatures to All Outgoing Messages check box and make sure that the signature is selected as the default. (*Note:* Select the Don't Add Signatures to Replies and Forwards check box if you want to add your signature only occasionally.)

4. Click OK to save the signature.

5. To manually add a signature to an open e-mail message, choose Insert➪Signature and select a signature from the list that appears to insert it (see Figure 17-26).

 If you intend to use the signature on every e-mail, be careful that you don't include information you don't want everybody to know, such as your home address. Signatures aren't intended to be novellas — keep it short. Include contact information you want everybody to have; your affiliation (such as Pastor, Unitarian Church); or your thought for the day.

Figure 17-25: The Signatures tab of the Options dialog box

Figure 17-26: Inserting a signature manually

Create Mail Rules

1. You can create rules for how Windows Mail handles messages. For example, you can create a rule that all messages from your grandchildren be automatically placed in your Grandchildren folder. Choose Tools⇨Message Rules⇨Mail.

2. In the resulting New Mail Rule dialog box (see Figure 17-27), select a check box in the Select the Conditions for Your Rule area to set a Condition for the rule. For example, if you want all messages that contain the word *Sale* in the subject line to be moved to a Junk Mail folder, select the Where the Subject Line Contains Specific Words option.

3. Mark the Select the Actions for Your Rule check boxes to choose rule actions. In the example in Step 2, for instance, you would select the Move It to the Specified Folder option.

4. In the Rule Description area, click a link (the colored text). To continue the example shown in Figure 17-28, you click the phrase Contains Specific Words. Fill in the specific information for the rule in the dialog box that appears (see Figure 17-28 for an example). For the second item in this example, click the word specified and select a folder for matching messages to be moved to.

5. Click OK to return to the New Mail Rule dialog box. Fill in the Name of the Rule text box with a name that you can recognize and then click OK.

 After you create a rule, open the Message Rules dialog box (choose Tools⇨Message Rules⇨Mail) and then click the Modify button in the Message dialog box to make changes to the rule, or click the Remove button to delete it.

Figure 17-27: The New Mail Rule dialog box

Figure 17-28: Creating a Rule description

Send E-Mail to Groups Safely

1. Spammers can co-opt recipient addresses from e-mails and are especially attracted to e-mails with multiple addresses. To protect your friends' privacy, follow this procedure for addressing e-mails to groups. Choose Start⇨All Programs⇨Windows Mail.

2. Click the Create Mail button on the Windows Mail tool-bar to create a new, blank e-mail form.

3. Click the To: or CC: link. This displays the Select Recipients dialog box for entering recipients' addresses (see Figure 17-29). Enter all recipient addresses in the Bcc field. Doing so keeps all addresses private from the entire group of recipients. Click OK when you've entered all addresses.

4. Click in the Subject text box and type a concise yet descriptive subject such as Club Meeting or Holiday Visit.

5. Click in the message text area and type your message.

6. Click the Send button. The message will be sent, and privacy has been protected.

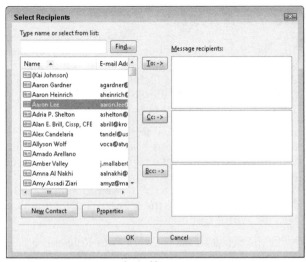

Figure 17-29: Entering Cc and Bcc addresses

Connecting with Others

Chapter 18

*Y*ou may have grown up in a world where people held conversations in person, by writing letters back and forth, or over the phone, but the Internet has revolutionized the way people connect. Today, people can communicate over the Internet in many ways. You can interact using a variety of technologies and with a variety of devices. You can enter text messages into your computer or cell phone that people receive immediately or whenever they get around to checking for messages. You can post an online journal called a *blog* (which stands for Web log) or read others' blogs. You can find people with like interests in a huge number of topics ranging from genealogy to investing to online gaming. When face-to-face communication just isn't possible, you will find the Internet a wonderful way to share ideas, information, and support.

In this chapter, you get advice about the following ways to interact with others online:

➠ Communicate via text messages and Internet phone calls.

➠ Post your thoughts to a discussion board or chat in real time in a chat room.

➠ Create your own online journal, called a *blog*, for others to visit.

Get ready to . . .

Use Instant Messaging to Send a Message

1. One way to connect directly with people who are online at the same time as you is by using an *instant messaging* (IM) program such as Windows Live Messenger, Yahoo! IM, or AIM, AOL's instant messaging program. First open a messaging program such as Windows Live Messenger. You can download this program from `http://get.live.com`.

2. Choose Start⇨All Programs⇨Windows Live⇨Windows Live Messenger. In the resulting window (see Figure 18-1) you can do any of the following:

Button	Location	What It's Good For
Add a Contact	1	Click this button to create a list of people with whom you want to connect. This list is called a *buddy list* or *contact list*. When you sign in to your IM program and your instant messaging window appears, it lets you know who's online. If any of your buddies are online, you can then send text messages back forth to each other.
Share	2	In addition to text messages, you can share links to journal entries and photos in Windows Live Spaces.
See Who Is Online Right Now	3	Click this button to see any contacts you've added who are online at the moment.
Send a Message to a Mobile Device	4	This allows you to send a message to a mobile device.

1   2   3   4

Figure 18-1: Windows Live Messenger

Carefully consider who you allow on your IM contact list. Whoever is on that list knows every time you go online. Stick to friends and family and people you want to chat with on a regular basis.

Make a VoIP Phone Call

VoIP stands for Voice over Internet Protocol. You can use this technology to make calls to anywhere in the world from your computer. You can also use a webcam along with VoIP to create a video phone system.

Here are the basic steps you should know for using VoIP:

➡ There are various VoIP providers, such as Skype and Vonage. Costs for signing up with these providers vary but are often much lower than paying a traditional phone company. Because there's no per call or per minute charge, the basic fee is usually paid for by your savings on long distance.

➡ When you sign up with a provider, you'll have to download software and make a test call using a microphone you connect to your computer.

➡ To use a VoIP service, you enter a list of contacts just as you do for instant messaging or e-mail. When you want to make a call, you choose a contact and click a button.

➡ You can make calls to other's computers equipped with VoIP or to a regular handheld or cell phone.

➡ VoIP services also offer features such as voicemail, caller ID, and call forwarding. If you don't want to be disturbed while working on your computer, you can block calls temporarily.

➡ Several sites, such as `http://voipreview.org`, can help you compare services before you sign up (see Figure 18-2).

Figure 18-2: Finding the right VoIP service for you

 Is your daughter living in another country? Check your provider's coverage area. Many allow international calls for no additional charges.

Post to a Discussion Board

A mainstay of online communication is *discussion boards*. A discussion board is a place where you can post written messages on a topic, and others can reply to you, or you can reply to their postings (and the postings might stay up there for years). Discussion boards are asynchronous, which means that you post a message (just as you might on a public bulletin board) and wait for a response. Somebody might read your message that hour or ten days or ten weeks after you post it. In other words, the response isn't instantaneous. The advantages of discussion boards are

Figure 18-3: Following threads in a discussion

➠ They allow you to give thought to your posting and spend time considering replies that others post to your discussion.

➠ They're organized in easy-to-follow *threads*, which organize postings and replies in an outline-like structure (see Figure 18-3), and you can review the comments of various participants as they add their ideas to the entire discussion.

 If pure text bores you, consider going to a video sharing site such as YouTube. Here people post videos instead of text, and you can comment on their postings. Another option is to include a link to a video in your discussion posting, which others in the discussion can click on to go to a posted video on a video sharing site.

Participate in a Chat

A *chat* is an online space where people can talk back and forth via text; when the chat is over, unless you save a copy, the text is gone. With chat, the interaction is in real time (synchronous) and resembles a conversation in text. Chat takes place in virtual spaces called *chat rooms*.

Chat has these advantages:

⟹ You can interact with others right away by typing your message and sending it. However, chat messages are usually rather brief to keep the conversation flowing (see Figure 18-4).

⟹ Several people can interact at once, though this can take getting used to as you try to follow what others are saying and jump in with your own quickly typed messages.

⟹ You can usually invite others to enter a private chat room, which keeps the rest of the folks who wandered into the chat room out of your conversation.

 An alternative to a chat room is using programs such as Skype to talk in real time over an Internet connection just as you would in a phone call, and even set up webcams so participants can see each other. Visit www.skype.com for more about their service.

Figure 18-4: Exchanging comments with others in a chat room

Set Up a Blog

The term *blog* comes from the phrase *Web log*. Blogs are essentially online journals or diaries in which people share their ideas and thoughts and others can comment on them. Both companies and individuals can create blogs. Figure 18-5 shows a blog at `www.look-both-ways.com`, which discusses how to stay safe online.

Here's some general advice about how to begin to explore the world of blogging:

➡ **Getting your own blog:** You can get a blog space from several sources, including your e-mail program such as Windows Live Hotmail or from a blog space service such as `www.blogger.com`. Creating a blog (see Figure 18-6) space is usually free and the sign up process is simple.

➡ **Considering your access options:** Be aware of the settings you make when creating a blog. Allowing public access to the blog means that anybody can listen in to your thoughts and emotions and pick up private information about you from your blog entries. You might be safer setting up to provide access only to those you know. Even if you post blog entries anonymously, some folks have figured out how to find out your real name, so limiting access to your blog entries is the safest approach.

➡ **Designing your blog's appearance:** Blog sites typically provide tools to help you easily design your space. You can choose whether to post a picture of yourself and what colors and fonts to use. You can also organize the layout of postings, archives of older postings, and responses.

➡ **Interacting with the blogging community:** You can search blog sites to find people with like interests. If another person's blog is open to the public, you can read and respond to comments posted there.

Figure 18-5: A popular blog on Internet safety

Figure 18-6: Creating a blog on `www.blogger.com`

Part V
Computer Maintenance and Security

Computer Maintenance

*T*his chapter covers tasks that are about as much fun as cleaning out your refrigerator. The fact is that computer maintenance might not be a barrel of laughs, but it keeps your computer running, so it has to be done. These are the types of tasks that help you keep your computer organized, in shape, and performing at its best.

The tasks in this chapter fall into two categories:

➡ **Performing basic maintenance:** These tasks help you keep your Windows house in order. To keep your system in shape, you can *defragment* your hard drive (take small fragments of files and consolidate them to make accessing them more efficient) or free up space on the drive. These tasks optimize how files are stored on your hard drive to make sure that you get the best performance from your computer.

➡ **Fixing common problems:** Windows has built-in features that help you troubleshoot hardware and software problems. The Hardware Troubleshooter takes you through a series of steps to isolate hardware malfunctions caused by hardware drivers, and the System Restore allows you to turn back the clock to a time when your software was working properly. By returning to a system restore point, you may undo newer settings that caused your system to act up or crash.

Get ready to . . .

Defragment a Hard Drive

1. *Defragmenting* reassembles data on your hard drive to use the space more efficiently. Many people recommend defragmenting your hard drive on a regular basis to keep your computer performing at its best. Choose Start⇨Control Panel⇨System and Maintenance and then click Defragment Your Hard Drive (in the Administrative Tools section).

2. In the resulting Disk Defragmenter window (see Figure 19-1), to the left of the Defragment Now button is a note about whether your system requires defragmenting or if regular defragmenting is set up to run automatically. To defragment now, click the Defragment Now button.

3. In the following Defragment Now dialog box (see Figure 19-2), select the drives to defragment and click OK. The message that appears tells you that Windows is defragmenting your drive and that it might take up to a few hours to complete. Windows shows you a progress window while you wait.

4. When the defragmenting process is complete, the Disk Defragmenter window shows that your drive no longer requires defragmenting. Click Close (the X in the upper right) to close the window.

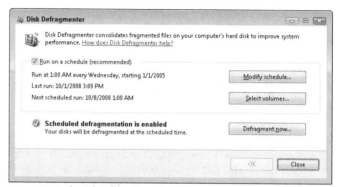

Figure 19-1: The Disk Defragmenter window

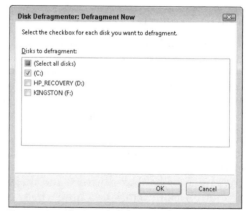

Figure 19-2: Choosing which drives to defragment

 To keep defragmenting from interfering with your work, try running it overnight while you're happily dreaming of much more interesting things. You can also set up the procedure to run automatically at a preset period of time, such as once every two weeks, by selecting the Run On a Schedule check box in the Disk Defragmenter window. A default schedule appears; to change it, click the Modify Schedule button and choose how often, what day, and what time to run the procedure. Of course, your computer has to be turned on for the scheduled defragmenting to occur.

 Remember: Disk defragmenting can take a while. If you have energy-saving features active (such as a screen saver), they might cause the defragmenter to stop or delay, so you might want to turn off the screen saver feature. (Choose Start⇨Control Panel⇨Appearance and Personalization and click the Change Screen Saver link.)

Free Up Disk Space

1. With all the little bits of data saved around your hard drive, there are some pieces that have become useless (little bits of files you deleted three years ago, for example). You can use a Windows tool to clean up your drive to remove that debris, which improves your computer's performance. Choose Start⇨Control Panel⇨System and Maintenance and then click Free Up Disk Space in the Administrative Tools.

2. In the dialog box that appears (see Figure 19-3), click the icon next to the kind of files you want to clean up. If you choose Files from All Users on This Computer, go to Step 3. If you choose My Files Only, choose the drives you want to scan from the Disk Cleanup: Drive Selection dialog box that appears and then proceed to Step 3.

3. The resulting dialog box shown in Figure 19-4 tells you that Disk Cleanup has calculated how much space can be cleared on your hard drive, and you also see a list of the suggested files to delete. (Those to be deleted have a check mark.) If you want to select additional files in the list to delete, click to place a check mark next to them, or deselected files if you want to keep them around. In most cases, whatever Windows proposes to delete is probably safe to delete, including fragments of long gone files and otherwise corrupted data you haven't accessed in a long time.

4. After you select all the files to delete (or accept the suggested files, which is probably just fine in most cases), click OK. The selected files are deleted.

 Click the View Files button in the Disk Cleanup dialog box to see more details about the files that Windows proposes to delete, including the size of the files and when they were created or last accessed.

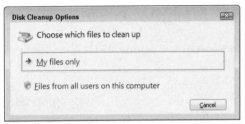

Figure 19-3: A Disk Cleanup dialog box

Figure 19-4: Viewing how much disk space can be freed by Disk Cleanup

 Though the Disk Cleanup process is pretty safe, if your computer starts behaving strangely after the cleanup, you might want to create a System Restore point before you run it. This feature saves periodic backups of your system, and you can use it to restore your computer to an earlier time. If Disk Cleanup causes any problems, choose Start⇨ Control Panel⇨Restore Files from Backup and then click the Restore Files button. Follow the wizard screens that appear to restore files to the restore point you created before you ran Disk Cleanup.

Use the Troubleshooter Tools

1. Choose Start⇨Help and Support⇨Troubleshooting Tools.

2. In the resulting Troubleshooting Tools window (see Figure 19-5), scroll down and click the appropriate link for any problem you're experiencing.

3. Follow the instructions that relate to your problem. (Figure 19-6 shows the results of using the System Information troubleshooting tool, as an example.)

4. After you solve the problem, click the Close button to close the Troubleshooting window. If you don't find a solution, consider using the Remote Assistance feature to get one-on-one help. (See Chapter 8 for more about this feature).

 You might also find help with the hardware drivers by going to the Device Manager (Start⇨Control Panel⇨Hardware and Sounds⇨Device Manager) and right-clicking a device. Choose Properties and then display the Driver tab to update or test a driver.

 Individual computer manufacturers may customize the help system so that your troubleshooting options and tools may differ depending on the computer you're using.

Figure 19-5: The Troubleshooting Tools window

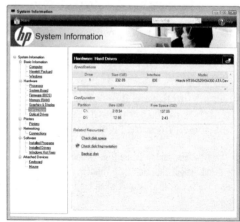

Figure 19-6: System information and tools to help you solve your problem

Create a System Restore Point

1. Choose Start➪Control Panel➪Backup Your Computer (under System and Maintenance).

2. In the Backup and Restore Center window, click Create a Restore Point or Change Settings under Tasks. The User Account Control might display a dialog box asking for your permission to continue; if so, click Continue.

3. On the System Protection tab of the System Properties dialog box that appears (see Figure 19-7), click Create.

4. In the resulting Create a Restore Point dialog box (see Figure 19-8), enter a description; this description is helpful if you create multiple restore points and want to identify the correct one. The current date is a logical option.

5. Click the Create button, and the system restore point is created and is available to you when you run a System Restore (see the following task for more about this.)

6. In the dialog box that appears telling you the restore point was created successfully, click OK and then click OK again to close the Control Panel.

 Before you install some software or make some new settings in Windows, create a system restore point. It's good computer practice, just like backing up your files, only you're backing up settings that work before you change them.

 A more drastic option than System Restore is to run the system recovery disc that probably came with your computer or that you created using discs you provided. However, system recovery essentially puts your computer right back to the configuration it had when it was carried out of the factory. That means you lose any software you've installed and documents you've created since you began to use it. A good argument for creating system restore points on a regular basis, don't you think?

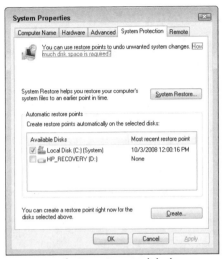

Figure 19-7: The System Properties dialog box

Figure 19-8: The Create a Restore Point dialog box

Restore the Windows System

1. Choose Start⇨Control Panel⇨Back Up Your Computer (under System and Maintenance).

2. In the Backup and Restore Center window, click Repair Windows Using System Restore in the Tasks list.

3. In the resulting System Restore dialog box (see Figure 19-9), click Next to use the suggested restore point; or click Choose a Different Restore Point and click Next, select a restore point, and click Next again.

4. In the next window that appears, click Finish to confirm the system restore point.

5. A dialog box confirms that you want to run System Restore. Click Yes.

6. The system goes through a shutdown and restart sequence, and then displays a dialog box that informs you that the System Restore has occurred.

7. Click OK to close the dialog box.

 System Restore doesn't get rid of files that you've saved, so you won't lose your Ph.D dissertation. System Restore simply reverts to Windows settings as of the restore point. This can help if you or some piece of installed software made a setting that is causing some conflict in Windows that makes your computer sluggish or prone to crashes.

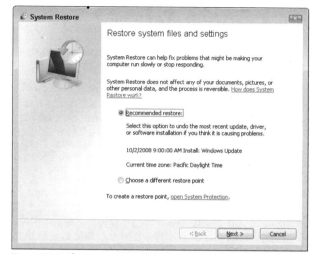

Figure 19-9: The System Restore dialog box

 Another cause of slow downs in your system could be malware that has downloaded to your computer. This type of software, which might be a virus or spyware, for example, can be detected and blocked by using antivirus and antispyware programs such as MacAfee, Spyware Terminator, or Windows Defender. See Chapter 20 for more about using Windows Defender.

Protecting Windows

Your computer contains software and files that can be damaged in several different ways. One major source of damage is from malicious attacks that are delivered via the Internet:

➡ Some people create damaging programs called **viruses** specifically designed to get into your computer hard drive and destroy or scramble data.

➡ Companies might download **adware** on your computer, which causes pop-up ads to appear, slowing down your computer's performance.

➡ **Spyware** is another form of malicious software that you might download by clicking a link or opening a file attachment. Spyware sits on your computer and tracks your activities, whether for use by a legitimate company in selling you products or by a criminal element to steal your identity.

Microsoft provides security features within Windows Vista that help to keep your computer and information safe, whether you're at home or travelling with a laptop computer.

In this chapter, I introduce you to the major concepts of computer security and cover Windows Vista security features.

Chapter 20

Get ready to . . .

Understand Computer Security

When you buy a car, it has certain safety features built in. After you drive it off the lot, you might find that the manufacturer slipped up and either recalls your car or requests that you go to the dealer's service department to get a faulty part replaced. In addition, you need to drive defensively to keep your car from being damaged in daily use.

Your computer is similar to your car in terms of the need for safety. It comes with an operating system (such as Microsoft Windows) built in, and that operating system has security features. Sometimes that operating system has flaws, and you need to get an update to keep it secure. And as you use your computer, you're exposing it to dangerous conditions and situations that you have to guard against.

Threats to your computer security can come from a file you copy from a disc you insert into your computer, but most of the time the danger is from a program that you downloaded from the Internet. These downloads can happen when you click a link, open an attachment in an e-mail, or download one piece of software without realizing that the malware is attached to it.

You need to be aware of the three main types of dangerous programs (called *malware*):

➡ A **virus** is a little program that some nasty person thought up to spread around the Internet and infect computers. A virus can do a variety of things, but typically it attacks your data, deleting files, scrambling data, or making changes to your system settings that cause your computer to grind to a halt.

➡ **Spyware** consists of programs whose main purpose in life is to track what you do with your computer. Some spyware simply helps companies you do business with track your activities so they can figure out how to sell you things; other spyware is used for more insidious purposes, such as stealing your passwords.

➡ **Adware** is the computer equivalent of telemarketing phone calls at dinner time. Once adware gets downloaded onto your computer, you'll get annoying pop-up windows trying to sell you things all day long. Beyond the annoyance, adware can quickly clog up your computer, so its performance slows down, and it's hard to get anything done at all.

To protect your information and your computer from these various types of malware, you can do several things:

➠ **You can buy and install an antivirus, antispyware, or antiadware program.** Programs such as McAfee Antivirus, Norton Internet Security from Symantec (see Figure 20-1), or the freely downloadable AVG Free from Grisoft can help stop the downloading of malicious files, and they can detect files that have somehow gotten through and delete them for you. Remember that after you install such a program, you have to get regular updates to it to handle new threats, and you need to run scans on your system to catch items that might have snuck through. Many antivirus programs are purchased by yearly subscription, which gives you access to updated virus definitions that the company constantly gathers throughout the year.

➠ **Some other programs such as Spyware Doctor from PC Tools combine tools for detecting adware and spyware.** Windows Vista has a built-in program, Windows Defender, that includes an antispyware feature. Windows Defender tools are covered later in this chapter.

➠ **You can use Windows tools to keep Windows up-to-date with security features and fixes to security problems.** You can also turn on a firewall, which is a feature that stops other people or programs from accessing your computer without your permission. These two features are covered in this chapter.

Figure 20-1: Norton Internet Security

Understand Windows Update Options

When a new operating system like Windows Vista is released, it has been thoroughly tested; however, when the product is in general use, the manufacturer begins to find a few problems or security gaps that it couldn't anticipate. For that reason, companies such as Microsoft release updates to their software, both to fix those problems and deal with new threats to computers that appeared after the software release.

Windows Update is a tool you can use to make sure your computer has the most up-to-date security measures in place. You can set Windows Update to work in a few different ways by choosing Start⇨All Programs⇨Windows Update and clicking the Change Settings link on the left side of the Windows Update window that appears. In the resulting dialog box (see Figure 17-2), you find these settings:

➡ **Install Updates Automatically:** With this setting, Windows Update starts at a time of day you specify, but your computer must be on for it to work. If you've turned off your computer, the automatic update will start when you next turn on your computer, and it might shut down your computer in the middle of your work to complete the installation.

➡ **Download Updates But Let Me Choose Whether to Install Them:** You can set up Windows Update to download updates and have Windows notify you (through a little pop-up message on your taskbar) when they're available, but you get to decide when the updates are installed and when your computer reboots (turns off and then on) to complete the installation. This is my preferred setting because I have control and won't be caught unaware by a computer reboot.

➡ **Check for Updates But Let Me Choose Whether to Download and Install Them:** With this setting, you neither download nor install updates until you say so, but Windows notifies you that new updates are available.

➡ **Never Check for Updates:** You can stop Windows from checking for updates and check for them yourself, manually (see the following task). This puts your computer at a bit more risk, but it's useful for you to know how to perform a manual update if you discover a new update is available that you need to proceed with a task (such as getting updated drivers or a language pack).

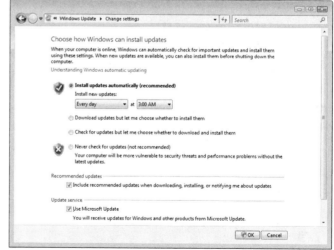

Figure 20-2: The Windows Update dialog box

Run Windows Update

1. No matter which Windows Update setting you choose (see the preceding task), you can run a manual update at any time. To do so, make sure you have an active Internet connection, and then choose Start➪All Programs➪Windows Update.

2. In the resulting Windows Update window, click Check for Updates. Windows thinks about this for a while, so feel free to page through a magazine for a minute or two.

3. In the resulting window, as shown in Figure 20-3, click the View Available Updates link.

4. In the following window, which shows the available updates (see Figure 20-4), select the check boxes for the updates you want to install. (It usually doesn't hurt to just accept all updates, if you have the time to download them all.) Then click the Install button.

5. A window appears, showing the progress of your installation. When the installation is complete, you might get a message telling you that it's a good idea to restart your computer to complete the installation. Click the Restart Now button.

 If you set Windows Update to run automatically, be forewarned that when it runs it might also automatically restart your computer to finish the update installation sequence. Although it displays a pop-up message warning that it's about to do this, it's easy to miss. Then you might be startled to find that whatever you're working on shuts down and your computer restarts when you least expect it.

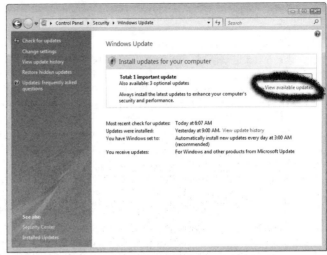

Figure 20-3: The View Available Updates link

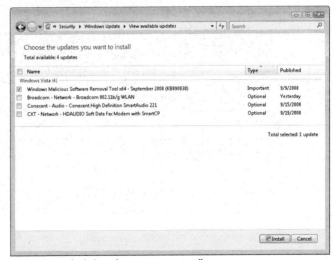

Figure 20-4: Check the updates you want to install

Enable the Windows Firewall

1. A *firewall* is a program that protects your computer from the outside world, preventing others from accessing your computer and stopping the downloading of dangerous programs such as viruses. With a firewall on, if you try to access sites or download software, you're asked whether you want to allow such access. Be aware, however, that you must turn on your firewall before you connect to the Internet for it to be effective. To turn on your firewall, choose Start➪Control Panel➪Check This Computer's Security Status.

2. In the Windows Security Center window that appears (see Figure 20-5), verify that the Windows Firewall is marked as On. If it isn't, click the Windows Firewall link in the left pane of the window and then click the Change Settings link in the resulting dialog box.

3. In the resulting Windows Firewall Settings dialog box (see Figure 20-6), select the On option and then click OK.

4. Click the Close button to close Windows Security Center and the Control Panel. Your firewall is now enabled and should stay enabled unless you go in and change the setting.

 Antivirus and security software programs might offer their own firewall protection and might display a message asking whether you want to switch. Check their features against the Windows Firewall features and then decide, but usually most firewall features are comparable. The important thing is to have one activated.

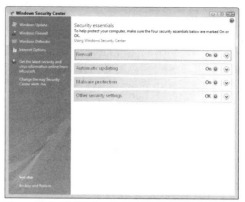

Figure 20-5: The Windows Security Center window

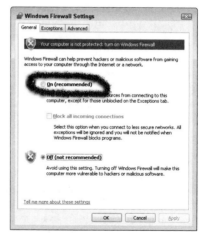

Figure 20-6: The Windows Firewall Settings dialog box

Run a Windows Defender Scan

1. If you use Windows Defender to detect spyware, you must run a *scan* of your computer system on a regular basis, which searches your computer for any problem files. You can run scans by setting up an automatic scan or by manually running a scan at any time. To make these settings choose Start⇨All Programs⇨Windows Defender.

2. In the resulting Windows Defender window, click the down-pointing arrow on the Scan button (see Figure 20-7).

   • **Quick Scan:** This runs a scan of the likeliest spots on your computer where spyware might lurk.

   • **Full Scan:** This scan checks every single file and folder on your computer and gives any currently running programs the once-over. However, be aware that during a Full Scan your computer might run a little more slowly.

   • **Custom Scan:** This scan allows you to customize where to scan. This is helpful if you suspect that a particular drive or folder is harboring a problem.

3. If you choose Quick Scan or Full Scan, the scan begins immediately. If you choose Custom Scan, you can click the Select button in the Select Scan Options dialog box that appears (see Figure 20-8). Then, in the Select Drives and Folders to Scan dialog box, select drives, files, and folders to scan. Click OK. Back in the Select Scan Options dialog box, click Scan Now.

4. When a scan is complete, a dialog box appears, listing any instances of spyware that were found and deleted or informing you that no spyware was found. Click the Close button to close the Windows Defender window.

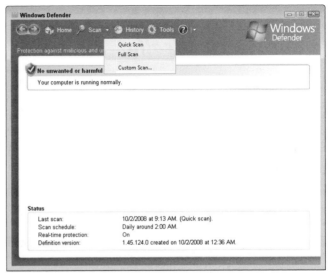

Figure 20-7: The Windows Defender window

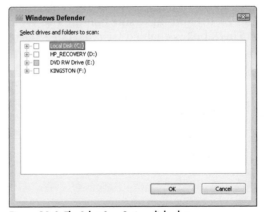

Figure 20-8: The Select Scan Options dialog box

Set Up Windows Defender to Run Automatically

1. If you prefer to have Windows Defender run on its own so you never miss a scan (a good idea, by the way), you can set it up to do so. Choose Start➪All Programs➪ Windows Defender.

2. In the resulting Windows Defender window, choose Tools➪Options. In the Options dialog box that appears (see Figure 20-9), select the Automatically Scan My Computer check box if it's not already selected and then choose the frequency, time of day, and type of scan from the drop-down lists.

3. To ensure that your scan uses the latest definitions for *malware* (a kind of spyware with malicious intent), select the Check for Updated Definitions before Scanning check box.

4. Scroll down to the bottom of the Options dialog box (see Figure 20-10) and make sure that the Use Windows Defender check box is enabled (selected) to activate the program.

5. Click Save to save your settings.

 If you want to exclude certain files or locations from the regular scans, you can use the Advanced Options in the Windows Defender dialog box. Click the Add button and browse for the location or file you want to exclude.

Figure 20-9: The Options dialog box

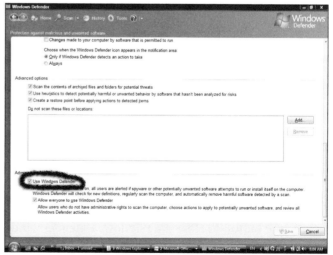

Figure 20-10: The Windows Defender check box selected

Require Logon to Close Screen Saver

1. Choose Start⇨Control Panel; click the Appearance and Personalization link (see Figure 20-11), and click Change Screen Saver.

2. In the resulting Screen Saver Settings dialog box (see Figure 20-12), select the On Resume, Display Logon Screen checkbox.

3. Click OK to save the new setting and close the dialog box.

 You can change settings for your screen saver by clicking the Settings button in the Screen Saver Settings dialog box. In the resulting dialog box, you can modify the style of the screen saver objects, the color scheme, and the size and resolution of the image.

 If you don't have a Windows Vista password set and you activate the Display Logon Screen feature nobody can turn off the screen saver without the password. But keep in mind, logon only requires a password only if one is set up for Windows Vista. Otherwise, you simply click your user name at the logon screen and disable the screen saver.

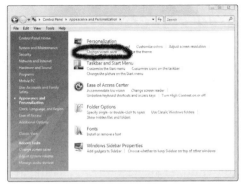

Figure 20-11: The Appearance and Personalization dialog box

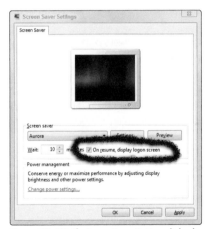

Figure 20-12: The Screen Saver Settings dialog box

Enable Shared Folders

1. You can allow other people on your network to view shared folders and files; first you have to enable this feature. Choose Start➪Network (see Figure 20-13) and click the Network and Sharing Center.

2. Click the arrow to the right of the Public Folder Sharing option in the Sharing and Discovery area of this dialog box (see Figure 20-14).

3. Click the radio button labeled Turn On Sharing So Anyone With Network Access Can Open Files.

4. Click Apply, and then click the Close button to close the dialog box.

 To find out more about using Windows Explorer to locate and work with files, see Chapter 8.

 You can right-click a file or folder, choose Share, and then click the Share button in the resulting dialog box to share it with others on the network. Only shared folders and files will be available to others once you have made the settings in this task.

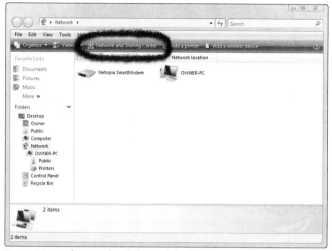

Figure 20-13: The Network and Sharing dialog box

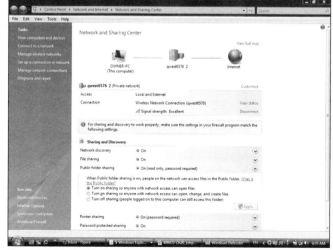

Figure 20-14: The File Sharing settings

Set Up Trusted and Restricted Web Sites

1. Choose Start⇨Control Panel⇨Security.

2. In the resulting Security dialog box, click the Internet Options link.

3. In the resulting Internet Options dialog box, click the Security tab (see Figure 20-15) and then click the Trust Sites icon.

4. Click the Sites button; in the resulting Trusted Sites dialog box (see Figure 20-16) enter a URL for a trusted Web site in the Add This Web Site to the Zone text box.

5. Click Add to add the site to the list of Web sites.

6. Repeat Steps 5–6 to add more trusted sites. Note that if you choose Restricted Sites in Step 4, you use a similar procedure to add sites you do not trust.

7. When you're done, click OK twice to close the dialog boxes.

 Note that if the Require Server Verification (https:) for All Sites In This Zone check box is selected in the Trusted Sites dialog box, any Trusted site you add must use the `https` prefix, which indicates that the site has a secure connection.

 You can establish a Privacy setting on the Privacy tab of the Internet Options dialog box to control which sites are allowed to download cookies to your computer. *Cookies,* tiny files that are used to track your online activity, recognize you when you return to a source site. *Trusted sites* are the ones that you allow to download cookies to your computer even though the privacy setting you have made might not allow any other sites to do so. *Restricted sites* can never download cookies to your computer, no matter what your privacy setting is.

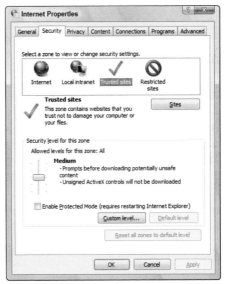

Figure 20-15: The Internet Options dialog box, Security tab

Figure 20-16: The Trusted Sites dialog box

Index

• Q •

• R •

• Z •